W9-BBE-150

Tomatoes & Mozzarella

100 Ways to Enjoy This Tantalizing Twosome All Year Long

Tomatoes &
Mozzarella

Hallie Harron and Shelley Sikora

Photographs by Richard Eskite

The Harvard Common Press • Boston, Massachusetts

The Harvard Common Press
535 Albany Street
Boston, Massachusetts 02118
www.harvardcommonpress.com

Copyright © 2006 by Hallie Harron and Shelley Sikora
Photographs copyright © 2006 by Eskite Photography

All rights reserved. No part of this publication may be reproduced or transmitted in any form
or by any means, electronic or mechanical, including photocopying, recording, or any information
storage or retrieval system, without permission in writing from the publisher.

Printed in China
Printed on acid-free paper

Library of Congress Cataloging-in-Publication Data

Harron, Hallie.
    Tomatoes & mozzarella : 100 ways to enjoy this tantalizing
twosome all year long / Hallie Harron and Shelley Sikora.
    p.   cm.
Includes index.
ISBN 1-55832-299-X (hardcover : alk. paper)
    1. Cookery (Tomatoes)   2. Cookery (Mozzarella cheese)
I. Sikora, Shelley.   II. Title.
TX803.T6D66 2006
641.6'5642–dc22

                          2005023814

ISBN-13: 978-1-55832-299-8
ISBN-10: 1-55832-299-X

Special bulk-order discounts are available on this and other Harvard Common Press books.
Companies and organizations may purchase books for premiums or resale, or may arrange a
custom edition, by contacting the Marketing Director at the address above.

Book design by rlf design

*Photographer: Richard Eskite; photo assistant: Brad Ryder; producer: Juliann Harvey;
food styling: Andrea Lucich; food styling assistant: Caitlyn Hicks; prop styling: Carol Hacker*

10 9 8 7 6 5 4 3 2 1

To San Pasqual,

patron saint of all cooks and kitchens

−HH

Acknowledgments

When two people come together and make magic out of
two ingredients, the result is a cookbook that explodes
with the passion of global cooking. It takes a village,
though, and we want to thank all those who believed in
our vision. Stacey Glick, our agent, always was a bright
light throughout the project. Thank you to Mary Evans,
dear friend and colleague, for eating tomatoes month after
month, and for all the moral support every step of the
way. Jay and Fran London, where would we be without
your thoughtful comments and meticulous testing and
retesting? And a big thank-you goes to Annette Ramseyer
in Vaison-la Romaine, France, whose kitchen skills and advice were constantly welcome. Thanks to both of our hus-
bands, Brian Harron and Bob Sikora, for constant support
and for making our lives easier as we pushed along month
after month. Thank you both for loving tomatoes and
mozzarella as much as your wives do. Last, thank you to
our inspirations, Shelley's mother, May Pino-Acquaro,
with whom we wish we could still cook, her father, Phil,
and Brooke Sikora, for their constant love and support.

Contents

Introduction

Anyone who has ever tasted just-picked, juicy tomatoes still warm from the sun combined with soft, milky mozzarella knows without a shadow of a doubt that this is simply heaven on a fork. This divine match has pleased the Western world for generations. Over the past decade cooks all over the globe have discovered new ways to dress up these old soul mates. Decked out in global flavors and garnishes, cloaked in pastry, and accessorized in everything from soup to dessert, it's safe to say the world has gone way beyond the classic and simple pairing of the two in *insalata Caprese*.

Two's company, and it is hard to imagine two better-suited partners on a plate than mozzarella and tomatoes. We learned this firsthand while spending time in the City of Light. On some summer days, Paris can be compared to living in a steamy convection oven: it's hot, it's wet, and it burns. Appetites wane, and light salads and easy cooking are often the only possible meal choices. For us, one mozzarella salad at a local bistro followed another in a Parisian tea salon. Mozzarella and tomatoes were on the menu at the fancy neighborhood three-star restaurant. And so it went. Each experience brought different tomato varietals, presentations, and garnishes. Cool, warm, molded, layered, pureed: it was all tomatoes and mozzarella. As fall approached, late-harvest tomatoes fell into soups, casseroles, and gratins. Despite being in a different form, tomatoes and mozzarella were still everywhere. Arriving back home with bulging notebooks, we became determined to create a seductive volume on the beloved mozzarella-and-tomato marriage.

So read on, and be prepared to wrap your arms around all seasons and all forms of the famous fruit (yes, it's a

fruit) and cheese. In the pages that follow, you'll wander the globe from the American Midwest to the Mediterranean Riviera, covering every time of the day from breakfast to late-night snacks, from January through December.

The recipes include everything from quick no-cook meals to dishes designed for the serious enthusiast who finds joy in quality time in the kitchen. The only prerequisite for this voyage is a consuming passion for Romas, heirlooms, cherries, and beefsteaks, not to mention bocconcini and ovalini. Beautiful, luscious tomatoes, that is, and creamy, soft, voluptuous mozzarella cheese. You'll soon be slicing, grating, shredding, dicing, and savoring both all year round in appetizers, soups, salads, grills, casseroles, and breads.

So come stroll with us through farmers' markets, wander through the Midwest and San Francisco and New York, then hop a plane and visit Paris bistros, Greek tavernas, and Italian trattorias. Let us share with you our experiences and give you the tools to enjoy tomatoes and mozzarella at home, 365 days a year.

The Dish on Tomatoes and Mozzarella

an you trust a tomato in January? What do you plant where and when? What's in a name? Heirlooms? Hybrids? Romas? Plums? Cherries? Beefsteaks? The tomato world has exploded into a huge industry that can seem like a big maze.

And that soft, milky mozzarella cheese, seemingly so mild and benign: Do we buy cow or buffalo, and, by the way, does that mean cheese from the great Montana buffalo? If we buy fresh mozzarella, how do we store it so we maximize its freshness for the longest period of time? And what's the fresh kind supposed to be used for, anyway, instead of the "regular" kind?

The following is a brief primer on how to search out the best for the season and tips on what to use when, so that you will be able to make the most of the recipes in this book.

Tomato Talk

Fresh tomatoes are the ones that people justifiably argue over, debate the various merits of, and wax poetically on. Let's start with the basics.

Tomatoes from the Store and Farmers' Market

Most regular grocery store tomatoes are commercially produced hybrids. These are tomatoes that cannot reproduce by themselves. They've been crossbred for marketable characteristics such as greater fruit production, longer shelf life, and better disease resistance, which often results in a loss of flavor. That said, there are some delicious hybrids to be had out there.

So which variety should you use for which purpose? The varieties are endless, and you should do some taste-test experimentation with the types in your local supermarket to see what you like best. When we recommend a specific kind of tomato in our recipes, we suggest you use it if at all possible. When we just say *tomatoes,* use whatever variety looks best when you do your shopping.

Plum tomatoes are considered the basis of good sauces, purees, and tomato pastes because of their meaty pulp, thick skin, and lack of juice. The red varieties are still the most common, although you'll see both yellow and orange plum tomatoes. Their thick flesh makes for good slicing, and the reduced pulp makes plum tomatoes an excellent canning tomato.

There are dozens of varieties of plum tomatoes. By far the most common is the Roma tomato. Amish Paste, Napoli, and the famous San Marzano pear-shaped tomatoes are common plum tomato seeds. When you purchase fresh plum tomatoes in your supermarket, you are buying whichever particular variety is most available in your area due to heartiness and shelf life.

Flavorful plum tomatoes are widely available year-round, which is why we chose to use them often in our recipes. We have even found them in January in Minnesota—and they were darn good! If you wish, canned plum tomatoes can be substituted during the winter months for use in sauces, pastas, casseroles, and other baked dishes, but for salads and other recipes that call for raw tomatoes, it's best to use fresh.

Grape, cherry, and pear tomatoes are those juicy little mouthfuls that can be as sweet as candy. These are good both raw and cooked. Used raw in salads and in pasta sauces and other sauces, they add a sweet yet acidic taste with an eye-catching appearance. Good-quality grape and cherry tomatoes, in particular, are widely available year-round. In the warm months, look for all colors and shapes.

Beefsteak tomatoes, those large, luscious, and juicy fruits, are available in all colors. These are the ones that you just slice and eat, lightly grill, or use in all manner of summer salads. Big Boy, Better Boy, and Early Boy are some of the well-known beefsteak hybrids.

In addition to the hybrids, you will sometimes see heirloom tomatoes in your local market, particularly in whole-foods markets and farmers' markets. An heirloom tomato is an open-pollinated variety (which means it can reproduce without human intervention) that is at least 50 years old. There are several types. "Commercial" heirlooms are open-pollinated varieties that were brought into the market before 1940. "Family" heirloom tomato seeds are just that; they've been passed down through a family. Sometimes two heirlooms are combined to produce a "created" heirloom.

The light, creamy flesh of the Brandywine, the deep red French heirloom Marmande, and the Russian variety Paul Robeson are heirloom tomato favorites. Some of the grape and cherry heirloom darlings are Blondkopfchen, Isis Candy, and the tiny Sweet 100s, which you may see in stores elegantly still on the vine. You'll find these names sprinkled throughout the recipes. If heirloom tomatoes aren't available in your local supermarket or farmers' market, vine-ripened, locally grown, organic fruit will be the most flavorful substitution.

Growing Tomatoes in Your Home Garden

The tomato, hands down, is the most revered summer vegetable. Many varieties are suited to the small home yard or large container or patio garden. Some are easy to grow, and some varieties require more patience and time. Today, dozens of seed catalogs with mouthwatering photos of plump, colorful tomatoes are available for the taking. If you want to grow your own tomatoes, be sure to choose plants that will grow in your planting zone. Our best advice is to consult your local county agriculture extension office to find out about varieties that are hardy in your area.

Both heirloom and hybrid tomatoes are popular with home gardeners, and it is possible for the home grower to produce a delicious crop with either type. For a broad collection of tomatoes, seek out the heirloom Rainbow of Tomatoes collection, which features Dona (red), Moonglow (orange), Church (pink), Brandywine (red-yellow), Black Prince (deep purple), and Green Zebra (light green–striped).

Bush tomato varietals grow low to the ground, while other tomato plants require staking or caging. As a staked plant, tomatoes require a relatively small amount of space and may produce 8 to 10 pounds of fruit per plant. Bush varietals don't require staking or caging, but they produce less fruit, as the fruit tends to fall or grow on the ground as it gets heavier and thus is more subject to rot and disease.

Tomato plants will develop long roots along the stem and may be set deeply in the soil. Tomatoes are warm-weather plants and are quite sensitive to low night temperatures, so plant them when the last danger of frost has passed. You can start seeds indoors, under growing lights, or if you are lucky enough to have a climatized greenhouse, they may be planted in some areas as early as February or March. Start seeds indoors four to six weeks before planting the seedlings outside. Tomatoes can be grown in many different soil types and respond well to both commercial and organic fertilizers.

And after a summer of tending your garden, when the

Extra Tomato Tips

For optimum flavor, leave tomatoes out on the counter. Refrain from refrigerating them if possible. If they are not totally ripe, a kitchen windowsill at 62° to 69°F is ideal for ripening the fruit. Leaving tomatoes at room temperature before cooking them is a standard recommended practice, to ripen them and to maintain their sugar. After a dish has been prepared, either with chopped or cooked tomatoes, most times it is fine, and preferable, to refrigerate the dish to keep it fresh.

Tomatoes should smell like tomatoes. If yours are lacking in aroma, put them back on the sill until they are fragrant yet still firm.

For slicing beefsteak tomatoes, use a serrated knife. It makes even slices and keeps the juice in the tomato, not on the counter.

If you are using whole canned tomatoes and need them to be broken up, try using kitchen scissors right in the can to break them apart before adding them to the recipe.

Indian summer gives way to the chill of fall, what's left? You are bound to have some green tomatoes on the vine. Use these in pies and savory crumbles, and for good old fried green tomatoes.

Canned Tomatoes

When fresh tomatoes aren't the best option, it's time to head to the supermarket shelves. Today there are several brands of canned tomatoes that are excellent for all-around use, and canned tomatoes come in many different forms, such as chopped, whole, and ground peeled. You'll find also fire-roasted tomatoes, plain or spiced with green chiles, which make a wonderful spicy pasta sauce. Some plum tomatoes are actually packed in thick tomato juice, which can be a bonus in recipes when time is short. Imported San Marzano plum tomatoes are an excellent choice any time intense tomato flavor is required, and they make a great substitute for fresh plum tomatoes in many cooked dishes. A variety of brands now offer tomatoes that have been enhanced with herbs such as rosemary, basil, and marjoram, as well as garlic. Bingo! They give you instant sauce and unending resources for delicious meals. Our favorite brand overall is Muir Glen, but try different brands to find your own favorite.

Sun-Dried Tomatoes

Sun-dried tomatoes provide extremely intense flavor. It takes about seven pounds of fresh tomatoes to produce one pint of the sun-dried product. This fact accounts for the added expense for these precious red gems. They are usually made from Roma tomatoes and either commercially oven dried or dehydrated. Sun-dried tomatoes may be purchased dried or preserved in oil.

Dried tomatoes, sold in small packages or in bulk, must be rehydrated in water or broth before using. The sun-dried tomatoes in oil can be chopped or slivered and used as is. You can use whichever type you prefer, but the bonus with the latter is the fabulous flavor that seeps into the oil. You can use the oil to enhance salad dressings, as a marinade for grilled meats, or brushed over creamy mozzarella or bread.

Sun-dried tomato paste is also available in a tube, which is a convenient, no-fuss way to add tomato flavor to dishes. Last, commercially available sun-dried tomato pesto, also in tubes or in jars, is a flavorful combination of tomatoes, garlic, Parmesan cheese, and olive oil that can act as an instant mop on the grill or as a pasta sauce or salad dressing base.

A Healthy Note

It stands to reason that something as beautiful, sensuous, and delicious as the tomato would have some health benefits. Homegrown varieties have almost twice the amount of vitamin C as the commercial ones. There are also healthy doses of vitamin A, calcium, and iron, and all tomatoes are low in calories and fat free. Cooked tomatoes were most recently in the news for their lycopene, a nutrient that has been widely acclaimed for its cancer-fighting qualities.

Making Your Way to the Right Mozzarella

What exactly is "fresh mozzarella"? This is a traditional Italian cheese made from either cow's milk or water buffalo's milk and stored in water. The *mozzarella di bufala,* originally from the area surrounding Naples, Italy, is creamy white, with a paper-thin rind and a slightly tangy taste. Fresh cow's milk mozzarella is a little milder in

Fresh and Canned Tomato Equivalents

One pound of tomatoes equals about 3 globe tomatoes, 8 plum or Roma tomatoes, 30 cherry tomatoes, or approximately 2 cups chopped tomatoes.

One 28-ounce can of tomatoes equals about 4 cups fresh chopped tomatoes, with their juice.

One 15-ounce can of tomatoes equals about 2 cups fresh chopped tomatoes, with their juice.

One cup of canned diced or chopped tomatoes equals about 1½ cups fresh chopped tomatoes, with their juice.

flavor than the buffalo type. Both kinds have a soft texture and are delicious.

For the imported variety you may need to visit an Italian food store, but domestic varieties are readily available at supermarket deli counters. Whether you use domestic or imported fresh mozzarella depends on what you are using the cheese for and on your pocketbook. We think it is best to use imported fresh mozzarella, buffalo if possible, when the cheese is the star of the recipe, as in many salads and some main courses. In cooking, whether to top casseroles or as a filling or other mixed-in ingredient of some kind, domestic is perfectly suitable. Ultimately, it depends on what is available in your area and how much you want to spend, as imported mozzarella will always be a bit more expensive than domestic. There are more good-quality domestic varieties appearing all the time.

Fresh mozzarella should be used as soon as possible; however, it does keep for up to three weeks, depending on the manufacturer. Store it in the water it comes in, and if you keep it for several days, change the water every other day.

Different sizes of fresh mozzarella are given different names. The tiniest round mouthfuls, about the size of a cherry and ⅓ ounce each, are called *ciliegine*. Next are *bocconcini,* which are about 1 inch in diameter and about 2 ounces each. These smaller sizes are often sold marinated in olive oil and spices, as well as plain in water. The larger ovals, about 4 ounces each, are called *ovalini*. You may sometimes see these in marinated form, but most often they are sold plain, in water. Some delicatessens stock a fresh mozzarella that has been braided for an elegant appearance. These soft, milky cheeses are best marinated, served as is on their own, or as the star of an appetizer or salad plate. This is also the type of mozzarella that is traditionally used on classic Neapolitan pizza—that is, the kind made in Naples. So fresh mozzarella does work for melting; however, it melts in one spot and doesn't spread out.

The shredded or brick domestic cheeses are what provide that oozy, melted result we are more accustomed to. (Nevertheless, an advantage to using fresh mozzarella on pizza is that it doesn't get rubbery as it cools.)

A sturdier and much drier mozzarella can also be purchased in the cheese section of the supermarket. This is generally labeled "fresh" mozzarella; however, it is not stored in water and is much firmer and more elastic in texture, and drier and less delicate in flavor, than fresh mozzarella. It is best used as a melting cheese in casseroles, on pizzas, and as toppings and in stuffings for roasted or grilled foods. Look for high-moisture mozzarella, sometimes called whole-milk mozzarella. The balls, wrapped in plastic, come in different sizes, with the standard being 6 to 8 ounces, and this cheese is also available in shredded form. Along with many other domestic mozzarellas, the whole-milk variety is a cow's-milk cheese and is easy to find in most grocery and specialty stores.

Part-skim mozzarella, also called low-moisture mozzarella, is firmer still in texture than the whole-milk variety and is the cheese to use when you need a uniform shredding cheese that will melt evenly. Many shredded varieties are part skim, but it is also sold in balls and bricks and sliced in packages.

In recipes where we specifically call for fresh mozzarella, we do recommend that you use that if at all possible. If the recipe calls simply for "mozzarella cheese," you may use whatever kind you prefer.

Some mozzarella has been smoked. In Italian groceries you may see it advertised as *mozzarella affumicata*. You'll find an imported variety called scamorza, which is excellent sliced as part of an antipasto or cheese platter. Domestic versions are just called smoked mozzarella. Both give an earthy, meaty touch to casseroles, gratins, and stuffings.

Homemade Mozzarella

If you want to experiment, try making your own fresh cheese. It's amazingly easy, actually. Some Italian and specialty food stores sell mozzarella curd, which is the basis for fresh mozzarella.

Makes about ½ pound cheese

1 pound fresh mozzarella curd, thinly sliced
2 gallons water
  Coarse kosher salt
  Rubber gloves
2 quarts ice water

1. Place the curd in a large heatproof bowl. Heat the water in a large pot over high heat to 120°F. Season generously with salt and pour the hot water over the curd. Using a wooden spoon, stir the mixture until the curd begins to pull apart. Put on the rubber gloves, then begin to bring the curd together by gently pulling and shaping the pieces by hand into 2- to 3-inch balls. As the cheese is formed (it will hold together and look like the balls you buy), plunge it into the ice water.

2. When the cheese has cooled, refrigerate it in slightly salted water for up to 3 days.

Breakfasts and Brunches

Move over, Bloody Marys! This almost frozen concoction is a wonderful way to welcome guests on a warm and sunny Sunday morning. The best way to prepare it is to freeze the tomatoes for about a half hour before blending; that way they will be well chilled but still manageable in the blender. The vodka is optional. Teetotalers will be just as happy, as the sweetness of the tomatoes along with the pungent horseradish and spicy Tabasco is a winning combination on its own. Mini-pearl tomatoes are an heirloom variety, whimsically named after comedienne Minnie Pearl.   **Serves 4**

Morning Tomato Smoothie

3   cups almost frozen ripe
     mini-pearl or grape tomatoes

⅓ cup fresh lime juice

1   tablespoon crème-style
     horseradish

2   teaspoons sugar

     Tabasco sauce to taste

     Sea salt to taste

4   ounces vodka (optional)

4   bocconcini mozzarella balls
     (about 8 ounces)

4   celery sticks with leaves

1. Place the tomatoes, lime juice, horseradish, and sugar in a blender. Blend for 1 minute on high to completely pulverize the tomato skins. Taste, and season with Tabasco and salt. Add the vodka, if desired, and blend for 10 seconds.

2. Attach 1 bocconcini to each celery stalk with toothpicks. Pour tomato mixture into glasses and garnish each with the celery.

Buy a package of imported grissini, or Italian breadsticks, and arrange them in a large water glass for a crunchy garnish. Such a little touch makes for a dramatic presentation! Or serve this with thin slices of baguette. Also, look for capote capers. These are one notch above the standard supermarket variety and are much more flavorful.   **Serves 4**

Tomato, Mozzarella, and Smoked Salmon Carpaccio

1 pound ripe plum tomatoes, very thinly sliced

8 ounces fresh mozzarella cheese, cut into 16 thin slices

Coarse sea salt and freshly ground black pepper to taste

2 ounces cold-smoked salmon, cut into ¼-inch strips

1 tablespoon large capers

2 tablespoons extra-virgin olive oil

1 tablespoon store-bought prepared basil pesto

1. Place the tomato slices on a medium-size serving platter. Intersperse the mozzarella slices between the tomatoes. Lightly season with salt and pepper. Place the strips of salmon in a crisscross pattern over the tomatoes and cheese. Scatter the capers over the top.

2. Whisk together the olive oil and pesto in a small bowl. Brush the mixture over the tomatoes, cheese, and salmon. Serve immediately or refrigerate for up to 8 hours. Serve at room temperature.

Here's an upgrade on classic deviled eggs. The result is a light, colorful, and, most important, scrumptious little way to start a brunch party. Feel free to vary the color of the tomatoes. The final dish will be spectacular if you have access to yellow, red, and orange plum tomatoes. If you have a grapefruit spoon at home, it works great for scooping out the tomato halves.

Makes about 30 tomatoes

Deviled Tomatoes

4	hard-boiled eggs, peeled
¾	cup shredded mozzarella cheese
2	tablespoons sour cream (low-fat okay)
1	tablespoon fresh Italian parsley, minced
2	teaspoons Dijon mustard
1	teaspoon cider vinegar
	Sea salt and freshly ground black pepper to taste
3 to 5	drops hot sauce of your choice
¾	pound small ripe plum tomatoes (about 15 tomatoes), cut in half lengthwise
15	bocconcini mozzarella balls, cut in half

1. Separate the whites from the yolks of the eggs and finely mince both separately. Place half of the whites and all of the yolks in a large bowl. Stir in the shredded mozzarella, sour cream, parsley, mustard, and vinegar. Season with salt, pepper, and hot sauce.

2. Using a spoon, gently scoop out the seeds from each tomato half. Place a heaping teaspoon of the egg mixture in each tomato half. Top the tomatoes with the remaining egg whites and garnish each one with a bocconcini half. Serve immediately, or cover and refrigerate for up to 2 days before serving. This is best eaten at room temperature.

The delightful bonus in this soufflé is that when cooked, the molten inside makes for an instant sauce when it is cut open. This will serve four people as an elegant appetizer that you can serve right from the baking dish. If you want to serve two as a main course, simply accompany the soufflé with a green salad and some bread and you've got a delectable lunch. Use your microwave to warm the milk. It saves a step and a pot! **Serves 4**

Heirloom Tomato Soufflé with Mozzarella

2 tablespoons finely grated Parmesan cheese

3 tablespoons unsalted butter

3 tablespoons all-purpose flour

1¾ cups milk, warmed

½ teaspoon sea salt

¼ teaspoon freshly ground black pepper

Pinch of nutmeg

5 large eggs, separated

1 tablespoon store-bought prepared basil pesto

2 cups chopped ripe tomatoes

1 cup shredded mozzarella cheese

1 pound cherry tomatoes on the vine, for garnish

1. Preheat the oven to 400°F. Oil an 8-cup soufflé dish. Dust the bottom and sides with the Parmesan cheese.

2. Heat the butter in a large saucepan over medium heat and let it brown slightly. Stir in the flour. Cook for 3 minutes over medium heat, stirring occasionally. The mixture will turn a light beige color. Whisk in the warm milk. The mixture will bubble and thicken quickly. Stir in the salt, pepper, and nutmeg, and remove from the heat to cool slightly.

3. In a small bowl, whisk together the egg yolks and pesto. Stir this into the pan along with the chopped tomatoes and mozzarella. The batter will be lumpy. In a separate bowl, beat the egg whites with a pinch of salt until stiff. Fold one-quarter of the whites into the batter and mix gently but thoroughly to lighten the mixture. Then fold in the remaining whites very gently.

4. Pour the batter into the prepared soufflé dish and place in the oven. Immediately lower the temperature to 375°F and bake for about 35 minutes. The center of the soufflé should still be very slightly wobbly. Remove the dish and place it on a napkin-lined serving plate. Garnish the plate with the cherry tomatoes on the vine, and serve immediately.

Soft, succulent, ripe tomatoes baked with a buttery, crunchy topping make for a stellar brunch dish. If you have a pretty earthenware pan that can be brought from the oven to the table or buffet, so much the better. A springform, soufflé, or oval gratin pan will also work quite well.

Serves 4 to 6

Savory Roasted Tomato Crumble

3 pounds ripe plum tomatoes, cored and quartered

3 garlic cloves, thinly sliced

3 5-inch sprigs fresh thyme

2 6-inch sprigs fresh rosemary

Sea salt and freshly ground black pepper to taste

2 tablespoons extra-virgin olive oil

For the crumb topping

¾ cup all-purpose flour

½ cup (1 stick) unsalted butter, cut into small pieces

½ cup fresh bread crumbs

½ cup grated Parmesan cheese

¼ cup pine nuts

1 cup shredded fresh mozzarella cheese (about 3 ounces)

1. Preheat the oven to 300°F. Oil a roasting pan.

2. Place the tomatoes in the pan and scatter the garlic, thyme, and rosemary over them. Season with salt and pepper and drizzle the olive oil over the top. Cover and bake for 1½ hours. Remove the pan from the oven, discard the herb sprigs, and set aside to cool. Raise the oven temperature to 375°F.

3. To make the crumb topping, place the flour, butter, and bread crumbs in a food processor and pulse until the butter has been reduced to pea-size bits. Transfer the mixture to a large bowl and stir in the Parmesan cheese and pine nuts.

4. Oil a 9-inch springform pan. Remove the tomatoes from the roasting pan with a slotted spoon and place them in the springform pan. Cover with the crumb topping, pressing the topping down gently with your fingers. Bake for 45 minutes, or until golden brown.

5. Remove the tomatoes from the oven and turn the oven setting to broil. Top with the shredded mozzarella and broil for about 5 minutes, or until the cheese has melted and is lightly speckled. Cool slightly and serve hot.

Loosely based on the classic tarte Tatin from the French Tatin sisters, this elegant tart is remarkably easy. Meaty Roma, or plum, tomatoes make for the prettiest and most uniform look. Make sure to let the tart rest for at least 15 minutes before inverting to prevent the crispy crust from becoming soggy.

Serves 4

Tomato Tarte Tatin

¼ cup sugar

¼ cup red wine vinegar

12 ripe plum tomatoes (about 2 pounds), cored, quartered, and seeded

1 tablespoon minced fresh oregano leaves

2 small shallots, minced

2 tablespoons olive oil

Sea salt and freshly ground black pepper to taste

1 sheet prepared puff pastry

4 ounces fresh mozzarella cheese, thinly sliced

1. Preheat the oven to 375°F. Oil a 7-inch-round, at least 3-inch-deep, baking dish.

2. Heat the sugar and vinegar in a small saucepan over medium-high heat. When the liquid boils, cook for 3 to 5 minutes, or until syrupy. Set aside.

3. Place the tomatoes in a large bowl. Add the oregano, shallots, olive oil, salt, and pepper and blend gently. Arrange a layer of tomatoes on the bottom of the baking dish in a circular pattern. Carefully spoon the remaining tomatoes on top. Pour the vinegar-sugar syrup over the tomatoes. Bake for 1 hour. Remove from the oven and cool slightly.

4. Cut the puff pastry in a circle, placing it on the top of the pan and over the tomatoes, without crimping it down. It should just reach the outer edges of the baking dish. Bake for 20 to 25 minutes, or until golden. Remove from the oven and cool for at least 15 minutes.

5. Invert the tart onto a serving platter and arrange the cheese slices on top in a circle pattern. Serve warm or at room temperature.

As a child living on the island of Mallorca, Hallie used to wander the fields that separated her family's tiny postage stamp of a village from the sea. No big hotels then! Occasionally, a villager working with his donkeys would share his morning snack, Pan Bali. Forty-five years later, this morning treat of fresh tomatoes and garlic rubbed on hearty bread still exists. Pan Bali is offered for breakfast all over Catalonia in small, modest hostels as well as in posher, well-known hotels. Enjoy the do-it-yourself experience of making Pan Bali, and pass platters of ham or sausage to go with it.   **Serves 6**

Catalan Tomato Bread

6 slices day-old country-style bread, sliced ½ inch thick, toasted or grilled

3 small garlic cloves, peeled and halved

3 large ripe tomatoes, cored and halved

Extra-virgin olive oil for drizzling

Red wine vinegar for drizzling

Sea salt to taste

6 ⅓-inch-thick slices of fresh mozzarella cheese (about 6 ounces), arranged on a plate

Place the warm bread on a serving platter. On another large platter, place a half clove of garlic on each tomato half. Bring cruets of oil, vinegar, and salt to the table, along with the cheese. To eat, rub the garlic onto the grilled bread and then smear the tomato half over the garlic. Place the cheese on top and sprinkle with a little more oil and vinegar. Season with salt and serve immediately.

Here's a unique waffle recipe for a lazy Sunday morning. If you wish, you can make the waffles ahead and crisp them with the cheese at the last minute. To expand on the corn theme, you could serve a light corn soup or a crispy green salad with additional corn kernels sprinkled over the top. If you're hosting a spice-loving crowd, the very piquant Chunky Tomato Chutney (page 165) would be a great alternative to the mild salsa. **Makes about 8 waffles**

Corn Waffles with Mozzarella and Summer Salsa

1½ cups all-purpose flour

1¼ cups cornmeal

2 teaspoons baking powder

½ teaspoon baking soda

1 teaspoon salt

1 cup fresh or frozen and defrosted corn kernels

2 large eggs plus 1 egg yolk

2½ cups buttermilk

2 cups shredded mozzarella cheese

Ultimate Summer Salsa (page 41)

1. Preheat the oven to 375°F.

2. In a large bowl, mix together the flour, cornmeal, baking powder, baking soda, salt, and corn. In a medium-size bowl, beat together the eggs and buttermilk. Stir the wet ingredients into the dry ingredients and mix well.

3. Heat a waffle maker and cook the waffles according to the manufacturer's instructions. Place the cooked waffles on a baking sheet. Sprinkle each with about ¼ cup of the cheese and bake for 5 minutes, or until the cheese has melted. Spoon the tomato salsa over the top and serve immediately.

Crepes are fun both to make and eat. Cut into half-moons and stuffed with a creamy tomato and mozzarella mixture, they can be served either as part of a brunch buffet or as finger food. The big bonus is that the crepes can be made and frozen up to one month in advance, making the final dish assembly a 1-2-3 snap.

Makes 36 crepes

Crepes with Minty Tomatoes and Mozzarella

18 Foolproof Crepes
    (recipe follows)

1   pint firm red grape tomatoes,
    quartered

2   tablespoons crème fraîche or
    sour cream

2   tablespoons minced
    fresh mint

    Sea salt and freshly ground
    black pepper to taste

16 thin slices of fresh
    whole-milk mozzarella
    cheese (about ¾ pound)

2   tightly packed tablespoons
    minced fresh Italian parsley

1. If you have made the crepes in advance, be sure to thaw them in the refrigerator for 1 day before using them. In a medium-size bowl, mix together the tomatoes, crème fraîche, mint, salt, and pepper.

2. Cut each crepe in half. Place a generous teaspoon of tomato filling in a crepe half, and then a thin slice of cheese. Fold the outsides of the crepe toward the center to enclose the filling. Place it seam-side down on a large serving platter. Repeat with the remaining crepe halves. Sprinkle the top of the platter with the parsley. Serve immediately at room temperature.

Foolproof Crepes

Makes about 36 crepes

Frozen, these keep well for more than a month. To freeze, stack and wrap them well in plastic packages. Thaw the packages overnight in the refrigerator before opening them to make sure the crepes do not tear.

   6 large eggs
  ⅔ cup half-and-half
1¼ cups milk (low-fat okay)
   1 cup water
   2 cups all-purpose flour
   2 tablespoons unsalted butter, melted
   1 tablespoon minced fresh basil leaves
   1 teaspoon salt
2½ tablespoons brandy or Cognac
   2 teaspoons lemon zest

   1. In a large bowl, mix together all the ingredients until smooth. Let the batter rest for 20 minutes or up to 1 day, covered, in the refrigerator.

   2. Heat a nonstick 7-inch crepe pan or small skillet over medium-high heat. Coat the pan lightly with butter. Add 3 tablespoons of the batter and quickly tilt the pan to coat the bottom of the skillet as evenly as possible. Cook the crepe just until set, about 1 minute. Turn the skillet upside down onto a clean surface. The crepe will slip right out.

   3. Repeat with the remaining batter. Be careful not to stack the crepes until they are completely cool.

Here's a fantastic savory twist on the American dessert classic. It makes a whimsical brunch or lunch dish. For the best texture and flavor, it is best to make and serve these shortcakes the day you bake them.

Serves 6

Summer Shortcakes with Tomatoes and Mozzarella

For the shortcakes

1½ cups all-purpose flour

½ cup cornmeal

2 tablespoons sugar

1 tablespoon dried Italian seasoning

2 teaspoons baking powder

¾ teaspoon sea salt

½ teaspoon baking soda

6 tablespoons cold unsalted butter, cut into ½-inch pieces

1 cup plus 2 tablespoons buttermilk

1 cup diced small ripe red tomatoes (about 5½ ounces)

1 small shallot, minced

1 teaspoon dried Italian seasoning

1½ tablespoons extra-virgin olive oil

1 tablespoon balsamic vinegar

½ teaspoon sea salt

¼ teaspoon freshly ground black pepper

1 pound fresh mozzarella cheese, cut into 6 thick slices

½ cup sour cream or plain yogurt (low-fat okay)

1. Preheat the oven to 400°F. Line a baking sheet with parchment paper and lightly oil the paper.

2. Place the flour, cornmeal, sugar, Italian seasoning, baking powder, salt, and baking soda in the bowl of a food processor and pulse to combine thoroughly. Add the butter and pulse into a grainy mixture. Add 1 cup of the buttermilk and pulse into a soft dough. *(continued)*

Summer Shortcakes with Tomatoes and Mozzarella

(continued)

3. Remove the dough from the processor and place on a well-floured surface. Roll the dough into a ½-inch-thick rectangle and cut out 3-inch rounds using a biscuit or cookie cutter. Reroll the scraps as necessary to use all of the dough. Place on the prepared pan and brush the tops with the remaining buttermilk. Bake for 10 to 12 minutes, or until browned.

4. While the shortcakes bake and cool, make the topping by placing the tomatoes, shallot, Italian seasoning, olive oil, vinegar, salt, and pepper in a large bowl. Mix well and set aside.

5. To serve the shortcakes, split each cake horizontally. Place a slice of the mozzarella cheese on the bottom half, and top with about ½ cup topping. It is fine if the topping slightly spills over onto the plate or platter. Spoon about 1 tablespoon of the sour cream over the topping, and place the other biscuit half on top. Serve immediately.

Having an Italian affair? Why not bring the Italian flag to the table? These incredibly easy savory pancakes are a unique way to serve the classic tomato and mozzarella combination. Try creating a pinwheel effect by sandwiching the warm flapjacks between overlapping layers of the ruby-red tomatoes and creamy cheese. For an equally tasty dish that is bursting with fresh green color, serve the pancakes layered with Green Zebra heirloom tomatoes. Bravo, and *buon appetito*! **Makes about 24 flapjacks, to serve 8**

Fresh Pea and Basil Flapjacks with Tomatoes and Mozzarella

2½ cups fresh green peas

2 tablespoons minced fresh basil

1 large egg plus 1 egg yolk

3 tablespoons quick-rising flour

Sea salt and freshly ground black pepper to taste

Canola oil for the griddle

8 ounces fresh mozzarella cheese, cut into ½-inch slices

8 large ripe red tomatoes, cut into ½-inch slices

Extra-virgin olive oil

1. Preheat the oven to 300°F.

2. Place 2 cups of the peas, the basil, the egg and egg yolk, and the flour in the bowl of a food processor. Season lightly with salt and pepper. Process until smooth. Remove to a medium-size bowl and add the remaining ½ cup peas.

3. Lightly oil a large nonstick griddle or skillet with canola oil and heat over medium heat. For each flapjack, spoon a generous tablespoon of the batter onto the griddle and cook for 2 minutes, or until lightly golden. Turn and cook for 1 minute. Place the finished flapjacks on a baking sheet and keep warm in the oven while you cook the remaining flapjacks. Oil the griddle as necessary.

4. Arrange the flapjacks, cheese, and tomatoes in an alternating pattern on a serving platter. Season with salt and pepper, drizzle with olive oil, and serve while the flapjacks are still warm.

This quick brunch dish uses only one large skillet. If you're making this for a party, sauté all the ingredients except the eggs, cilantro, and cheese up to three hours ahead. Then scramble the eggs at the last minute. This is fabulous with the Tomato-Avocado Salsa on page 156, but it's also great with store-bought salsa. Along with the salsa and tortillas, pass that pitcher of margaritas.

Serves 6

Tomato-Chile Scrambled Eggs with Smoked Mozzarella

2 tablespoons vegetable oil

1 large serrano chile, seeded and minced

1 medium-size green bell pepper, seeded and chopped

½ medium-size white onion, finely chopped

Sea salt and freshly ground black pepper to taste

1 store-bought roasted red bell pepper, thinly sliced

12 red grape tomatoes, halved

1 teaspoon ground cumin

3 6-inch day-old or dry corn tortillas, cut into ½-inch strips

1 dozen large eggs, lightly beaten

2 tablespoons finely chopped fresh cilantro leaves

1½ cups cubed smoked mozzarella cheese (4 ounces)

Tomato-Avocado Salsa (page 156) or store-bought salsa of your choice

6 8-inch fresh corn tortillas, warmed

1. Heat the oil in a large nonstick skillet over medium heat. Add the chile, bell pepper, and onion. Season lightly with salt and pepper and sauté for 3 to 5 minutes, or until the bell pepper and the onion have softened slightly. Add the roasted pepper, tomatoes, cumin, and tortilla strips. Sauté for 3 minutes.

2. Add the eggs to the pan and scramble, stirring constantly, until eggs are almost set. Stir in 1½ tablespoons of the cilantro and all of the cheese and cook for 30 seconds, or until the cheese begins to melt.

3. Place the eggs on a warm platter and sprinkle the remaining ½ tablespoon cilantro over the top. Serve immediately with the salsa and warm tortillas.

This frittata was loosely adapted from a delicious lunch we had near the large flower market in Nice, on the southern French border. The city is so close to Italy that although its inhabitants call this dish *trouchia*, it is an Italian frittata by all appearances. The key to success is to use freshly steamed chard and the sweetest tomatoes you can find. Depending on your crowd, serve it for brunch along with a well-chilled Provençal rosé or freshly squeezed orange, tangerine, or grapefruit juice.

Serves 4

Tomato, Swiss Chard, and Mozzarella Frittata

1 bunch Swiss chard, stemmed and chopped (about 2 cups)

5 large eggs

½ cup grated Parmesan cheese

2 tablespoons heavy cream

½ teaspoon sea salt

¼ teaspoon freshly ground black pepper

2 tablespoons olive oil

1 shallot, minced

1 garlic clove, minced

15 small cherry tomatoes, halved

¾ cup shredded mozzarella cheese

1 tablespoon fresh chives, minced

1. In a steamer basket set over boiling water, steam the Swiss chard for about 3 minutes. Drain and set aside.

2. Preheat the oven to broil. In a large bowl, whisk together the eggs, Parmesan, heavy cream, salt, and pepper.

3. Heat the olive oil in a medium-size skillet over medium heat and sauté the shallot and garlic for 2 minutes. Add the Swiss chard and cook for an additional 1 to 2 minutes. Top with the egg mixture and cook for 3 to 4 minutes, or until the bottom is slightly set and the top is still runny.

4. Arrange the tomatoes and cheese on top and broil for 2 to 3 minutes, or until the cheese is melted and speckled and the frittata is set. Remove from the oven and sprinkle the top with chives. Serve warm.

In this chic omelet, the fresh mozzarella stays firm. It has a lovely texture paired with the soft and silky smoked salmon. Regular mozzarella doesn't work nearly as well here. Note that if you want to make this for more than two people, double the recipe and use an 8-inch frying pan. We hesitate to make a larger-than-4-egg omelet, as it gets too hard to fold in half, so if you're interested in making this for a crowd, make several small ones and serve them as they are ready.

Serves 2

Smoked Salmon and Tomato Omelet

1	tablespoon unsalted butter
6	cherry or grape tomatoes, halved
2	large eggs, beaten
⅓	cup shredded fresh mozzarella cheese (about 1½ ounces)
1½	ounces smoked salmon, shredded or minced
1	tablespoon minced fresh chives

1. Heat the butter over medium heat in a small nonstick frying pan. Sauté the tomatoes for 3 minutes, or until slightly softened. Pour in the eggs and stir until they just begin to set, about a minute. Scatter the mozzarella, smoked salmon, and half of the chives over the omelet and cook for about a minute, or until the bottom of the omelet just starts to turn brown.

2. Fold the omelet in half and turn it out onto a plate. Sprinkle the remaining chives on top and serve immediately.

This classic Basque dish is as great for dinner as it is for breakfast or brunch. Traditionally, pipérade is made with thick slices of ham from Bayonne and seasoned with the hot peppers from Espelette, a tiny village known for its hot pepper festivals. Prosciutto is easier to find, as is cayenne pepper, and they make great substitutions.   **Serves 4**

Pipérade with Scrambled Eggs and Mozzarella

2   tablespoons olive oil

1   large onion, chopped

2   small garlic cloves, thinly sliced

Sea salt and freshly ground black pepper to taste

1   medium-size red bell pepper, cored, seeded, and cut into 1-inch strips

1   pound ripe tomatoes, halved and grated on the side of a box grater

8   slices prosciutto

4   large eggs, lightly beaten

½   cup mozzarella cheese cut into ¼-inch cubes (about 2½ ounces)

Pinch of cayenne pepper

1. Heat the olive oil in a medium-size skillet over medium-low heat. Add the onion and garlic and season with salt and pepper. Sauté for 8 to 10 minutes, or until the onion has softened. Add the bell pepper and cook for 5 minutes, then add the tomatoes and simmer for 15 to 20 minutes, or until most of the liquid has evaporated.

2. Meanwhile, place the prosciutto into a separate large skillet and brown it on both sides over medium-high heat.

3. When the vegetables are cooked, pour in the eggs and cheese. Season with cayenne pepper and lightly scramble until the eggs are softly set and the cheese is stringy. Spoon the mixture into 4 individual shallow bowls, and form a cross on top of each with two slices of prosciutto. Serve immediately.

Finger Foods, Cocktail Tidbits, and First Courses

These homemade crackers are far above and beyond any store-bought equivalents. Marinated mozzarella is sold in Italian markets and in the deli section of many large supermarkets. If you have trouble finding it, simply place regular bocconcini in a small bowl and top with a generous tablespoon of olive oil, a squeeze of fresh lemon juice, and a handful of freshly chopped basil or other herbs of your choice. **Serves 10 to 12**

Tomato Crackers for Tomatoes and Mozzarella

1½ cups all-purpose flour

½ cup shredded sharp yellow cheddar cheese

3 tablespoons store-bought prepared sun-dried tomato pesto

1 teaspoon sea salt

¼ teaspoon freshly ground black pepper

9 tablespoons cold salted butter, cut into small pieces

¼ cup sour cream (low-fat okay)

1 tablespoon extra-virgin olive oil

1 egg yolk

1 cup grated Parmesan cheese

1 pint cherry tomatoes

1 pound marinated bocconcini balls

1. Place the flour, cheddar cheese, pesto, salt, and pepper in the bowl of a food processor and pulse to mix thoroughly. Add the butter and process until the mixture has a coarse cornmeal-like texture.

2. In a small bowl, stir together the sour cream, oil, and egg yolk. With the machine running, add the liquid and process just until the dough holds together. Remove from the bowl and pat into a 7-inch disk, about 1 inch thick. Wrap the disk in plastic wrap and refrigerate at least 3 hours or overnight.

3. Preheat the oven to 375°F.

4. On a floured surface, roll out the dough into a ⅛-inch-thick circle. Cut out crackers using a 1¾-inch cookie cutter and place on a parchment paper-lined baking sheet. Press together and reroll any remaining scraps of dough. Sprinkle each cracker with a generous teaspoon of Parmesan cheese.

5. Bake the crackers for 13 to 15 minutes, or until lightly browned on top. Remove and let sit on the baking sheet for 5 minutes before removing them to a rack to cool thoroughly.

6. Place the crackers in a large bowl and serve with small bowls of tomatoes and mozzarella balls, with toothpicks on the side for spearing them. If you prefer, cut the tomatoes and bocconcini balls in half so that you can serve them on top of the crackers.

This almost-fat-free relish can best be described as "good, clean fun." It's great with tortilla chips or pita chips. And unlike traditional salsa, it really could be the major part of a vegetarian meal. For brunch, we love to serve it on fresh greens or over homemade corn waffles, eggs, or both. (It's the best corn waffle topper we've ever found.) For a spicier version, substitute a hot serrano or jalapeño chile for the Anaheim chile.   **Makes 3 cups**

Ultimate Summer Salsa

1	cup grape tomatoes, quartered
1¼	cups cooked black beans or one 15-ounce can, drained and rinsed
½	cup fresh corn kernels
2	large scallions, minced (white and green parts)
½	cup chopped fresh mozzarella cheese (about 2½ ounces)
1	medium-size Anaheim chile, seeded and diced
2	tablespoons fresh lime juice
	Sea salt and freshly ground pepper to taste

Mix together all the ingredients in a large bowl. Serve immediately, or store in an airtight container in the refrigerator for up to 3 days. Allow to come to room temperature before serving.

These rich, buttery packets of flavorful tomatoes and mozzarella are easily made ahead, frozen, and baked at the last minute for a very elegant appetizer guaranteed to impress. Serve them with champagne or a very dry white wine. **Makes 30 turnovers**

Crispy Tomozz Turnovers

7	tablespoons extra-virgin olive oil
1	medium-size onion, finely chopped
2	garlic cloves, minced
1	store-bought roasted red bell pepper, minced
¼	cup tightly packed minced fresh Italian parsley
⅓	cup sun-dried tomatoes preserved in olive oil, minced
1	cup ricotta cheese
1	large egg yolk, beaten
¾	cup shredded mozzarella cheese
5	tablespoons unsalted butter, melted
15	sheets phyllo dough, thawed if frozen

1. Heat 2 tablespoons of the olive oil in a large skillet and sauté the onion over medium heat for 3 to 5 minutes, or until softened. Add the garlic and sauté for 2 minutes. Remove from the heat and stir in the bell pepper, parsley, tomatoes, ricotta, egg yolk, and mozzarella.

2. Preheat the oven to 350°F.

3. Stir together the remaining 5 tablespoons olive oil and the butter in a medium-size bowl. Place 1 phyllo sheet on a work surface, and brush lightly with the oil-butter mixture. Top with a second sheet, and brush with the oil-butter mixture. Repeat with a third sheet. Cut the stacked sheets crosswise into 6 strips, each about 3 inches wide. Spoon 1 tablespoon of the filling in 1 corner of each strip. Starting at the filled corner, fold the pastry over the filling as if folding a flag; take the bottom right corner and fold it up to the left to form a half triangle, then take the covered pastry and flip it up to the right. Continue in this manner until a secure pocket is formed and the pastry is all rolled up. Repeat the process with the remaining pastry sheets, strips, and filling.

4. As the packets are completed, place them on a baking sheet (or place them in an airtight container and freeze for up to 1 month). Bake for 12 to 15 minutes, or until golden. If the turnovers have been frozen, bake them directly from the freezer for 18 to 20 minutes longer (for a total of 30 to 35 minutes). Serve hot or warm.

Here's a tasty tidbit that you'll find sold on the streets of Rome. The name means "telephone wires," because of the little strings of mozzarella that stretch out as you bite into these incredibly flavorful morsels of rice and cheese. Serve them as a finger food with the marinara as a dipping sauce. If you happen to have leftover cooked rice and tomato sauce in the refrigerator or freezer, you can make these suppli in less than 15 minutes.   **Serves 8**

Suppli

2   cups Arborio rice

¼   cup minced prosciutto

1   large egg, lightly beaten

1   8-ounce ball fresh mozzarella cheese, cut into 16 pieces

1½   cups fresh bread crumbs

1   quart canola oil, for frying

2   cups Marinara Sauce (page 139), warmed

1. Cook the rice according to the package directions. Let cool.

2. In a medium-size bowl, mix together the rice, prosciutto, and egg. Lightly wet your hands and flatten ¼ cup of the rice mixture in your palm. Place a piece of mozzarella in the center and press the rice around it on all sides, forming a small ball.

3. Place the bread crumbs in a shallow bowl. Roll the ball in the bread crumbs to coat it thoroughly, and set aside on a large plate. Repeat with the remaining rice and cheese to form 16 balls.

4. Preheat the oven to 300°F. Heat the canola oil in a small, deep saucepan or deep-fryer to 375°F. Line a baking sheet with paper towels.

5. Fry the suppli 2 to 3 at a time, depending on the size of the pot. Be careful not to overcrowd them. Fry until dark golden brown, about 3 minutes, and then remove and drain on the paper towels. Place the suppli in the oven to keep them warm as you continue to fry the remaining ones.

6. Serve immediately with the marinara sauce.

This is a great combination of the traditional Caprese salad and the classic stuffed mushroom. Depending on what size mushrooms you buy, you may have some leftover filling. If so, it makes a delicious sandwich spread on rustic Italian bread. The tomato mixture is also a welcome summer salad on its own. **Serves 8**

Stuffed Mushrooms with Minced Tomatoes and Mozzarella

4 large sprigs fresh Italian parsley

2 large sprigs fresh basil

2 large garlic cloves

2 plum tomatoes, cored and quartered

1¾ cups cubed fresh mozzarella cheese (about 8 ounces)

3 green onions, peeled and coarsely chopped (white and green parts)

½ teaspoon sea salt

¼ teaspoon freshly ground black pepper

1½ pounds large white mushrooms, stems removed

Extra-virgin olive oil

¼ cup grated Parmesan cheese

1. Place the parsley, basil, and garlic in a food processor and pulse to mince. Add the tomatoes, cheese, and green onions and pulse to mince. Be careful not to puree; the mixture should be chunky. Remove the filling to a bowl and add the salt and pepper.

2. Preheat the oven to 425°F.

3. Spray or brush the mushrooms with the olive oil and place on a parchment paper–lined baking sheet. Stuff the tomato-cheese mixture into the center cavities. Sprinkle with the Parmesan cheese and bake for 10 to 12 minutes, or until the mozzarella has melted and the mushrooms are hot. Serve slightly warm or at room temperature.

The very humble onion is taken to new heights when roasted and stuffed with nutty garlic and dressed up with fresh, colorful tomatoes, herbs, cheese, and balsamic vinegar.   **Serves 2**

Roasted Onion Cups with Tomatoes, Mozzarella, and Roasted Garlic

2 tablespoons extra-virgin olive oil

2 teaspoons balsamic vinegar

Coarse salt and freshly ground black pepper to taste

1 teaspoon lemon pepper

3 medium-size sweet red onions, unpeeled and halved

3 large garlic cloves

1 large ripe red or yellow tomato, finely chopped

⅓ cup diced fresh mozzarella cheese (about 2 ounces)

1 tablespoon minced basil

3 cups mesclun or spring garden salad mixture

1. Preheat the oven to 350°F.

2. Oil an ovenproof casserole dish large enough to hold all the onions. Mix together the oil and vinegar and season with salt and both peppers. Brush half of this mixture over the cut onion halves. Place each half, cut side down, in the casserole dish. Brush the garlic with the remaining seasoned oil and wrap in aluminum foil. Place the foil packet in the casserole. Roast for 45 minutes, or until the onions are very tender and the cut sides have darkened. Check to see that the garlic is soft. Remove the onions and garlic from the oven and let cool slightly.

3. Remove the centers from the onions, leaving the outside "cups" intact. Remove the onion skin. Finely chop the onion centers along with the roasted garlic. Place the chopped onion and garlic in a medium-size bowl and add the tomato and cheese, along with any pan juices from the onions. Add the basil and gently mix.

4. Fill the onion cups with the mixture. Place the greens on a large serving platter and top with the filled roasted onion cups. Serve at room temperature.

Once the cheese has marinated in the tomato vinaigrette (which can be done a day ahead of time), you can put together this elegant first course in two minutes. Use a box grater to grate the tomatoes.

Makes 8 crostini

Prosciutto-Draped Crostini

1 large ripe tomato, cored and grated

1 shallot, minced

2 teaspoons red wine vinegar

3 tablespoons extra-virgin olive oil

4 ovalini mozzarella balls (about 1 pound), halved

4 thick slices Italian country bread, halved

8 thin slices prosciutto

1 tablespoon minced fresh Italian parsley leaves

1. Whisk together the tomato, shallot, vinegar, and olive oil in a medium-size mixing bowl. Add the mozzarella, cover, and marinate for 1 hour at room temperature or for up to 1 day in the refrigerator.

2. To serve, lightly toast the bread halves and place on a platter. Top each piece of bread with 1 ovalini half. Drape 1 slice of prosciutto over the cheese and pour the remaining marinade over the top. Sprinkle a little parsley over each plate, and serve at room temperature.

You are likely to have some of the shrimp mixture left over after serving this dish; perfect for lunch another day. Buy a fresh baguette, slather the rest of the shrimp mixture on a large slab, and enjoy with a really cold beer. You will save time by purchasing cooked shrimp, but if you buy them raw, simply steam them for a few minutes before proceeding.

Makes about 16 bruschetta

Tomato-Shrimp Bruschetta

½ pound cooked medium-size shrimp, tails removed and deveined

1 garlic clove

1 tablespoon capers

¾ cup shredded mozzarella cheese

2 large plum tomatoes, diced (about ¾ cup)

1 large green onion, minced (white and green parts)

4 tablespoons olive oil

1 tablespoon balsamic vinegar

Sea salt and freshly ground black pepper to taste

1 day-old baguette, cut on the diagonal into ½-inch slices

1. Chop the shrimp into ½-inch pieces and place in a medium-size bowl. Mince the garlic and capers together and add to the shrimp. Add the cheese, tomatoes, green onion, 2 tablespoons of the olive oil, and the vinegar. Season to taste with salt and pepper. Set aside.

2. Preheat the oven to 375°F.

3. Brush the bread slices with the remaining 2 tablespoons of the olive oil and place on an ungreased baking sheet. Bake for 10 minutes, or until golden.

4. Spoon 2 tablespoons of the shrimp mixture onto each bread slice. Serve at room temperature.

Here is some black-tie barbecue. After the bruschetta, serve a very simple grilled chicken and potatoes, and the crowds will cheer. Make sure that the bread you use for this bruschetta is at least a day old. It should be sturdy and take a little effort to slice.   **Serves 8**

Grilled Bruschetta with Ovalini and Chilled Green Zebra Tomato Salad

For the salad

2 cups tightly packed arugula leaves (6 ounces)

3 large ripe Green Zebra heirloom tomatoes, thinly sliced

3 tablespoons slivered fresh basil

Fleur de sel or sea salt and freshly ground black pepper to taste

¼ cup very thinly sliced or shaved Parmesan cheese

¾ cup pitted, marinated Greek olives

Extra-virgin olive oil for drizzling

For the bruschetta

1 loaf day-old rosemary focaccia, halved lengthwise and sliced into 6-inch slabs

½ cup sun-dried tomatoes in oil, minced, plus ½ cup of the oil

4 ovalini mozzarella balls (about 1 pound), thinly sliced

1. To make the salad, place the arugula on a large serving platter and top with the tomatoes. Top with the shredded basil and season lightly with salt and pepper. Top the platter with the Parmesan cheese and sprinkle the olives over all. Drizzle the top of the salad with olive oil. Set it aside while you prepare the bruschetta.

2. Prepare a hot fire in a grill, or heat the oven to broil.

3. To make the bruschetta, brush the focaccia slices with about 3 tablespoons of the sun-dried tomato oil, and grill or broil until well toasted, 2 to 3 minutes per side. Top each slice with a generous tablespoon of sun-dried tomatoes and 2 slices of cheese. Place back on the grill or in the oven for about 30 seconds, or until the cheese begins to melt.

4. Drizzle the remaining sun-dried tomato oil over the bruschetta. Serve hot, with the salad alongside.

The combination of warm, soft ricotta and cold or room-temperature fresh mozzarella in this dish is really appealing. The cornmeal tarts are good piping hot, but if you want to make them ahead, they are quite respectable served slightly warm. If you wish to serve only a few at a time, warm them in a toaster oven. A toothpick is helpful for holding the bocconcini in place.

Makes 18 tartlets

Polenta Tartlets with Grape Tomatoes and Bocconcini

1½ cups water

½ cup coarse polenta

1 teaspoon salt

½ cup milk

2 tablespoons unsalted butter

¾ cup ricotta cheese

1½ tablespoons store-bought prepared sun-dried tomato pesto

½ cup quartered grape tomatoes (about 2½ ounces)

18 bocconcini mozzarella balls (about 2¼ pounds), at room temperature

1. Oil 2 mini-muffin pans and set them aside. Place the water, polenta, and salt in a medium-size pot and bring to a boil over medium heat. When the mixture boils, reduce the heat to medium-low and cook, stirring frequently, until thickened, 8 to 10 minutes. Stir in the milk and butter, remove the polenta from the heat, and let cool for 1 minute.

2. Spoon the polenta into the wells of the prepared pans. Using a small spatula, push the mixture up the sides of the wells to create tartlets. Let the polenta cool completely to firm up.

3. Preheat the oven to 350°F.

4. Mix together the ricotta, pesto, and tomatoes in a small bowl. Using a small knife if necessary, remove the tartlets from the pans and place them on a baking sheet. Spoon the tomato mixture into the cups and bake for about 5 minutes, or until the tartlets are slightly warmed. Remove them from the oven and serve topped with a bocconcini secured with a toothpick.

This savory quick bread is best served in thin slices with cocktails. Leftovers can be toasted with a nice chunk of fresh mozzarella melted over the top. Ovenproof silicone cake and loaf pans are widely available now, making it really easy to both remove the bread and to prep and clean up. For an elegant retro variation, old-fashioned Bundt pans work beautifully. Just adjust the cooking time accordingly; the tried-and-true method of inserting a wooden skewer to test if the bread is cooked works well here. **Serves 6 to 8**

Savory Cocktail Cake of Mozzarella and Tomatoes

1½ cups all-purpose flour

1 tablespoon baking powder

Pinch of salt and freshly ground black pepper

⅓ cup olive oil

½ cup sun-dried tomatoes in oil, julienned, plus 1 tablespoon of the oil

½ cup crème fraîche or sour cream

½ cup water

3 large eggs

¾ cup shredded mozzarella cheese

⅓ cup shredded Gruyère cheese

1 tablespoon capers, chopped

2 tablespoons tightly packed chopped fresh basil

1. Preheat the oven to 350°F. Oil a 9-inch loaf pan and set aside.

2. In a small bowl, mix together the flour, baking powder, salt, and pepper. In a medium-size bowl, whisk together the olive oil, sun-dried tomato oil, crème fraîche, water, and eggs. Mix in the flour mixture, then mix in all remaining ingredients, including the sun-dried tomatoes.

3. Pour the batter into the pan and bake for 35 to 40 minutes, or until golden brown and a wooden skewer inserted in the center comes out clean. Set on a cooling rack for 10 to 15 minutes before removing from the pan and slicing.

Spicy peppers bathed in olive oil are extraordinary when paired with garden tomatoes and mild fresh mozzarella. Prepare and bake the peppers several days ahead if you wish, and store them in the casserole dish. Then, just before serving, bring them to room temperature and layer the tomatoes and cheese over the top. Prepared store-bought basil oil can be substituted for the tomato oil if time is a factor. Both are excellent toppers for the dish.   **Serves 6**

Roasted Peppers with Tomatoes and Mozzarella

4   small ripe red tomatoes (about 1 pound), cut in half

4   yellow chiles, seeded and cut into 1/8-inch strips

2   medium-size green bell peppers

2   medium-size yellow bell peppers

2   medium-size red bell peppers

5   garlic cloves, slivered

1/3 cup extra-virgin olive oil

1   teaspoon sea salt

1/2 teaspoon freshly ground black pepper

1/2 teaspoon *herbes de Provence*

3   medium-size yellow tomatoes, cored and thickly sliced

3/4 pound fresh mozzarella cheese, sliced into 1/4-inch-thick slices

2   tablespoons Fresh Herb Tomato Oil (at right)

1. Preheat the oven to 400°F.

2. Grate the red tomatoes, cut side down, using a box grater. Oil a 14-inch gratin or oval baking dish. Make 3 layers of chiles, bell peppers, garlic, grated tomatoes, olive oil, salt, pepper, and *herbes de Provence*.

3. Cover the dish and bake for 45 minutes. Uncover and bake for another 45 minutes to 1 hour, or until the top of the dish is slightly dried and browned on top. Remove from the oven and cool to room temperature. Arrange the yellow tomato slices and cheese slices in a shingle pattern down the center of the dish. Spoon the tomato oil over the cheese and serve immediately.

Fresh Herb Tomato Oil

Makes 3 cups

2   large ripe red tomatoes, coarsely chopped

1   large bunch fresh basil, chopped

1   teaspoon dried thyme
    Pinch of cayenne pepper

3   cups extra-virgin olive oil

Place all the ingredients in a large bowl. Cover and set aside for 24 hours. Strain, and refrigerate in an airtight container for up to 1 month.

This colorful and flavorful combination of pistachios, tomatoes, and diced mozzarella reminds us of confetti. Look for pistachio oil in specialty shops. We have found the imported Leblanc brand to be rich and pure, with a subtle green color. All nut oils are fragile, so be sure to store them in the refrigerator so they'll last for months. To toast the nuts, put them on a pan in one layer in a 350°F oven for about 10 minutes.　　　　**Makes 12 canapés**

Pistachio Confetti Canapés

1 pint yellow and red cherry tomatoes, stemmed and quartered

1 tablespoon balsamic vinegar

½ cup pistachios, toasted

2 tablespoons pistachio oil or other nut oil, such as almond or hazelnut

¾ cup diced fresh mozzarella cheese (about 4 ounces)

12 ½-inch-thick baguette slices

Extra-virgin olive oil

1. Preheat the oven to 350°F.

2. In a large bowl, gently mix together the tomatoes, vinegar, pistachios, pistachio oil, and half of the cheese. Place in a serving bowl and sprinkle the remaining cheese over the top. Set aside.

3. Lightly brush the baguette slices with the olive oil and place on a baking sheet. Bake for 10 minutes, or until the bread is toasted but still slightly soft.

4. Place the bread in a napkin-lined basket. Serve immediately with the confetti and small spoons for scooping it onto the bread.

As part of a larger cheese platter or simply on its own, this cheese-and-tomato combo is ideal for an Italian wine tasting. Feel free to double or even triple the recipe for a large crowd. Spear the cheese with toothpicks and serve this with plenty of cocktail napkins, as the delicious sauce tends to drip.

Serves 6

Herbed Bocconcini with Sun-Dried Tomato Dipping Sauce

1 tablespoon smoky
ground paprika

1 tablespoon toasted
sesame seeds

1 tablespoon freshly ground
black pepper

1 tablespoon *herbes de Provence*

1 teaspoon sea salt

6 ounces fresh bocconcini
mozzarella balls, halved, *or*
6 ounces whole ciliegine
mozzarella balls

½ cup sun-dried tomatoes
in olive oil

½ cup tightly packed minced
fresh Italian parsley

½ cup grated Parmesan cheese

2 tablespoons fresh lemon juice

2 tablespoons extra-virgin
olive oil

1. Place the paprika, sesame seeds, black pepper, and *herbes de Provence* on small individual plates. Sprinkle ¼ teaspoon salt over each plate and mix with a small spoon. Divide the cheese evenly among the plates and roll the balls in the individual coatings. Set the cheese on a serving plate and place a toothpick in each piece of cheese.

2. Place the sun-dried tomatoes, parsley, Parmesan, lemon juice, and olive oil in a food processor or blender and puree into a smooth dipping sauce. Place in a small serving bowl alongside the cheese. Serve at room temperature.

These designer pizzas are light appetizers for an Italian summer supper. They are an anchovy lover's delight, but if you prefer, you can omit the anchovies and top the pizzas with grated Parmesan and a few chopped oil-cured olives. **Serves 4**

Portobello Pizzas

1 tablespoon extra-virgin olive oil

½ medium-size onion, chopped

1 garlic clove, thinly sliced

2 medium-size ripe tomatoes, cored and chopped

1 pint cherry tomatoes, halved

4 large portobello mushrooms, stems removed and chopped

½ teaspoon dried oregano

¼ cup white wine

Sea salt and freshly ground black pepper to taste

1 tablespoon thinly sliced fresh basil leaves

6 ounces fresh mozzarella cheese, thinly sliced into 8 pieces

8 small anchovy fillets

1. Heat the olive oil in a large skillet over medium heat. Add the onion and slowly sauté for 20 minutes until browned and caramelized. Add the garlic and cook for 30 seconds. Add the tomatoes, mushroom stems, oregano, and wine. Season lightly with salt and pepper.

2. Simmer the sauce for 20 minutes, then stir in the basil. Remove from the heat, cool slightly, and place in a blender. Puree until smooth.

3. Preheat the oven to 475°F. Spray a parchment paper– or aluminum foil–lined baking sheet with nonstick cooking spray.

4. Place the mushroom caps on the prepared pan. Spoon 3 tablespoons sauce onto each cap. Top each with 2 slices of the cheese and top with remaining sauce. Top each mushroom with 2 crisscrossed anchovies. Bake for 10 to 12 minutes, or until the cheese is bubbly. Remove, cool slightly, and cut each "pizza" into quarters. Serve warm.

The combination of creamy ricotta and slightly molten mozzarella is a rich treat to serve as a first course. You can prepare the custards and refrigerate them for up to a day before baking. For a more substantial meal, place the custard in four larger cups and serve as a light entrée with a green salad. You'll need to bake the larger cups an extra 10 minutes. Cold leftover custards are delicious the next day.

Serves 8

Baked Ricotta and Mozzarella with Olives and Grape Tomato Clusters

1 pound whole-milk ricotta cheese

½ cup grated Parmesan cheese

3 large eggs, lightly beaten

2 tablespoons store-bought prepared basil pesto

8 small bocconcini mozzarella balls

3 tablespoons extra-virgin olive oil

2 tablespoons fresh lemon juice

1 tablespoon minced chives

Sea salt and freshly ground black pepper to taste

2 cups arugula leaves

12 ounces grape tomatoes, on the vine and divided into 8 sections if possible

⅓ cup oil-cured olives

1. Preheat the oven to 400°F. Oil eight ¾-cup ovenproof custard or soufflé dishes.

2. In a large bowl, mix together the ricotta and Parmesan cheeses, the eggs, and the pesto. Fill each dish with a generous ⅓ cup filling and place on a baking dish or tray. Place a bocconcini in each cup and submerge it underneath the custard. Bake for 35 minutes, or until the tops are puffed and browned. Remove to a rack and cool for 20 minutes.

3. While the custards bake, whisk together the olive oil, lemon juice, and chives in a medium-size bowl. Season with salt and pepper. Toss the arugula and tomatoes in the dressing, making sure to keep the tomatoes on the vine.

4. Line 8 salad plates or a large platter with the arugula, leaving a space in the center for the custards. Divide the olives among the plates or place them around the edge of the platter. Place the custards in the center and top each with a small cluster of tomatoes. Serve immediately.

These ultra-simple and very tasty skewers are perfect to serve at a cocktail reception, where people are often standing and eating with their hands. If you like, make mini-brochettes with toothpicks and pile them high in a beautiful bowl. Before serving, place a small amount of your best olive oil in a clean spray bottle and spritz the tops of the brochettes. This will make the food glisten, for a nice presentation.   **Makes 12 brochettes**

Bocconcini Brochettes

12 bocconcini or ciliegine
mozzarella balls

1 tablespoon minced
fresh chives

1 tablespoon extra-virgin
olive oil

2 teaspoons fresh lemon juice

Sea salt and freshly ground
black pepper to taste

12 6-inch bamboo skewers

24 large fresh basil leaves

12 cherry tomatoes

1. In a medium-size mixing bowl, lightly mix together the cheese, chives, olive oil, and lemon juice. Season lightly with salt and pepper. Cover and marinate in the refrigerator for at least 1 hour, or overnight if you have time.

2. For each wooden skewer, thread onto the end 1 basil leaf, 1 tomato, another basil leaf, and 1 bocconcini. Place on a serving platter. Reseason with salt and pepper if desired. Serve at room temperature.

These unique packets make for easy summer entertaining. They can be served as is for a first course and are also delicious as part of a salad, served with a little lemon or tomato vinaigrette. Assemble them as much as a day ahead, if you wish, and bake them right at the last minute.

Serves 8

Papillotes of Tomato, Mozzarella, and Eggplant

1 large globe eggplant, cut into
   ½-inch lengthwise slices

2 tablespoons olive oil

2 large ripe plum tomatoes,
   each sliced lengthwise into
   4 thick slices

2 ounces fresh mozzarella
   cheese, sliced into 8 pieces

8 large basil leaves

1. Preheat the oven to 375°F.

2. Brush the eggplant with the olive oil and place on a parchment paper–lined baking sheet. Bake for 40 minutes, or until the eggplant is soft. Remove from the oven and cool. Raise the oven temperature to 425°F.

3. Cut each eggplant slice in half lengthwise, and place one slice over the other to form a cross. Place a slice of tomato in the center of each cross. Top with a slice of cheese and a basil leaf. Fold over the ends of the eggplant to enclose the filling and form a neat packet. Secure with a toothpick. Bake for 10 to 12 minutes. Serve hot or at room temperature.

Romesco sauce is a classic Catalan condiment that combines well with vine-ripened tomatoes and soft fresh mozzarella. Make the sauce up to a week in advance and then assemble the stacks just before serving. It's important to toast the nuts to bring out their flavor, and it's easy! Just place the nuts in a single layer on a baking sheet and bake at 350°F for about 12 minutes, until lightly colored. You can toast the bread for the sauce at the same time.

Serves 4

Tomato Stacks with Mozzarella and Romesco Sauce

4 medium-size ripe yellow or orange tomatoes, with stems attached to tops

Romesco Sauce (at right)

8 ounces fresh mozzarella cheese, cut into 4 slices

2 tablespoons store-bought basil-flavored olive oil

Sea salt to taste

Slice each tomato widthwise into 4 pieces. For each tomato, spread 1 tablespoon Romesco sauce on the bottom slice and cover with the second tomato slice. Top with a piece of cheese and cover with the third tomato slice. Spread the top of the third slice with another tablespoon of Romesco sauce and top with the last tomato slice (which is the top to the tomato, with its stem). Drizzle ½ tablespoon olive oil over each tomato and sprinkle the tomatoes with salt. Serve immediately.

Romesco Sauce

Makes about ½ cup

1 1-inch-thick piece hearty country baguette, brushed with olive oil and toasted

2 tablespoons olive oil

1 to 2 ancho chiles, to your taste, soaked for ½ hour in hot water, drained, and seeded

½ serrano chile, stemmed, seeded, and minced

2 garlic cloves, minced

(continued)

Tomato Stacks with Mozzarella and Romesco Sauce

(continued)

¼ cup toasted almonds
¼ cup toasted hazelnuts
1 large ripe tomato, cored and grated against the side of a box grater
1 tablespoon minced fresh Italian parsley
1 teaspoon red wine vinegar
  Sea salt to taste

In a medium-size skillet, sauté the bread over medium heat in 1 table-spoon of the olive oil until lightly golden. Remove and drain on paper towels. Add the remaining 1 tablespoon of oil to the skillet and sauté the ancho and serrano chiles for 3 minutes. Cool slightly, and place the chiles in the bowl of a food processor with the garlic. Process until smooth. Add the almonds, hazelnuts, tomato, parsley, vinegar, and sautéed bread and process just to mix. Season to taste with salt.

We first spied this loaf in the windows of the famous Fauchon charcuterie in Paris. Sold by the slice, it is beautifully wrapped in a piece of gold foil. What elegant picnic fare it made! At home, the terrine is easily assembled with garden tomatoes and fresh cheese, and can be presented much more casually. Serve this as a first course with a few tender lettuce leaves, olive oil, very thinly sliced baguettes, and a bottle of Sancerre.   **Serves 8**

Terrine of Mozzarella and Tomatoes

2	envelopes unflavored gelatin
½	cup water
½	cup white wine
	Pinch of cayenne pepper
1	pound fresh mozzarella cheese, sliced as thinly as possible
¼	cup store-bought prepared basil pesto
3	large red tomatoes, cored and sliced as thinly as possible
8	large fresh basil leaves, for garnish

1. In a small saucepan, dissolve the gelatin in the water, wine, and cayenne pepper over medium heat. When the liquid begins to simmer, remove from the heat and let cool.

2. Lightly oil a 9 × 3½-inch loaf pan. Line the bottom of the pan with mozzarella slices and top with 1 tablespoon of the pesto. Spread a layer of tomato slices on top. Continue making layers with the remaining cheese, tomatoes, and pesto, ending with the pesto. Pour the cooled gelatin over the top, cover, and refrigerate for at least 2 hours.

3. To serve, cut into 8 thick slices and place on individual plates or a large serving platter. Top each slice with a basil leaf.

This dish was inspired by major food enthusiast and favorite recipe tester Jay London. He tells us that although tortillas can be found served at room temperature at tapas bars all over Spain, this one he remembers from Barcelona is draped in a spicy saffron tomato sauce and is best served warm. The cooking time on the sauce will vary: fresh tomatoes will need 30 to 35 minutes, while canned tomatoes will cook in 25 to 30 minutes. Be sure to use Yukon Gold potatoes if you can find them. If not, substitute any nonstarchy, nonrusset potato.   **Serves 4**

Spanish Tortilla with Fresh Mozzarella and Saffron Tomato Sauce

¼ teaspoon saffron threads

4 tablespoons olive oil

½ small onion, finely chopped

2 cloves garlic, minced

1 pound ripe plum tomatoes, peeled and coarsely chopped, or one 14.5-ounce can whole plum tomatoes, coarsely chopped

Sea salt and freshly ground black pepper to taste

2 tablespoons chopped fresh Italian parsley

2 medium-size Yukon Gold potatoes, peeled

6 large eggs

1 ovalini mozzarella ball, cut into ½-inch slices

1. Preheat the oven to 350°F.

2. Soak the saffron threads in a small bowl with 1 tablespoon of very hot water. Set aside.

3. Heat 2 tablespoons of the olive oil in a medium-size saucepan over medium heat and sauté the onion until soft, about 10 minutes. Add the garlic and sauté 1 minute, or until the garlic is slightly softened and fragrant. Add the chopped tomato and the saffron, along with its soaking water, and season with salt and pepper to taste. Reduce the heat to a simmer and cook for about 30 minutes. Stir in the parsley.

4. While the sauce cooks, prepare the tortilla. Fill a medium-size saucepan with water and bring it to a boil. Quarter and dice the potatoes into ¼-inch pieces. Place them in the boiling water and cook for 3 to 4 minutes, or until just barely tender. Drain and rinse the potatoes in cold water. In a large bowl, beat the eggs and season with salt and pepper.

5. Heat 1 tablespoon of the olive oil in a medium-size nonstick, oven-safe omelet or sauté pan. Add the potatoes. Cook over medium-low heat for 3 to 5 minutes to remove any excess water. The potatoes should still be only lightly colored. Remove from the heat and add to the beaten eggs.

(continued)

Spanish Tortilla with Fresh Mozzarella and Saffron Tomato Sauce

(continued)

6. Add the remaining 1 tablespoon of olive oil to the sauté pan and pour in the egg-potato mixture. Cover and place in the oven for 15 to 20 minutes, or until the eggs have set. Remove the cover, adjust the oven temperature to broil, and cook the tortilla for 2 to 3 minutes, or just until very lightly browned.

7. Place ½ cup of the tomato sauce in a large ovenproof serving dish. Remove the tortilla from the pan, place it on top of the sauce, and cover it with the remaining sauce. Place the mozzarella slices over the sauce and broil for 2 to 3 minutes, or until the cheese melts. Cut the tortilla into wedges and serve warm.

Here's a variation on a Middle Eastern favorite. We saw this originally in the North California wine country town of Rutherford. The mozzarella takes on a slightly briny, delicious undertone from the preserved grape leaves. The crispy grilled packets are a beautiful contrast to the tomatoes and their creamy mustard vinaigrette. This is good California eating! Note that if the grape leaves are small, you can overlap two of them to form a tight packet. Look for them in jars in the same section of your supermarket as the olives and relishes. You can also broil the packets for about two minutes per side, though they will be missing that smoky grilled flavor.

Serves 4

Grilled Stuffed Grape Leaves with Tomatoes and Capers

8 large preserved grape leaves

8 ounces firm mozzarella cheese, cut into 8 equal pieces

6 tablespoons olive oil

1 heaping teaspoon *herbes de Provence*

2 large ripe beefsteak tomatoes, each cut into 4 thick slices

1 tablespoon capers

2 tablespoons fresh lemon juice

1 tablespoon Dijon mustard

1 tablespoon chopped fresh Italian parsley

½ teaspoon ground cumin

Sea salt and freshly ground black pepper to taste

1. Remove the grape leaves from the jar and place them on a flat surface with the inner vein facing up. Place a mozzarella slice on each leaf and fold in the sides and top to form a closed packet. In a small bowl, mix together 2 tablespoons of the olive oil and the *herbes de Provence*. Brush this over the packets. Place the packets on a large dinner plate and set aside.

2. Arrange the tomato slices on a large serving platter and sprinkle the capers around the platter. In another small bowl, whisk together the lemon juice, mustard, parsley, and cumin. Whisk in the remaining 4 tablespoons olive oil and season to taste with salt and pepper.

3. Prepare a hot fire in a grill. Grill the packets for 1 to 2 minutes on each side. While the packets are grilling, spoon the vinaigrette over the tomatoes. When the grape leaves are ready, they will look slightly charred. Remove them carefully with a spatula or tongs and place them on top of the tomatoes. Serve immediately, before the cheese has time to become firm again.

Salads for All Seasons

This incredibly easy-to-prepare salad lends itself to endless variation. Diced morsels of white fish, tuna, cooked chicken, or cannellini beans can be added for a heartier one-dish lunch. The mâche, often called lamb's lettuce, provides an elegant serving touch and is now available in many supermarkets. If you happen by a Middle Eastern market, buy a jar of the seasoned roasted red pepper relish known as ajvar, and substitute that for the red peppers for a slightly spicier version. **Serves 4**

Marinated Artichoke Salad

1 12-ounce jar marinated artichokes, quartered

2 tablespoons extra-virgin olive oil

1 tablespoon red wine vinegar

1 cup fresh mozzarella cheese cut into ½-inch chunks (about 4 ounces)

1 cup chopped ripe tomatoes (about 4 ounces)

½ cup grated Parmesan cheese

2 store-bought roasted red bell peppers, minced (about 2 tablespoons)

2 tablespoons minced fresh Italian parsley

1 garlic clove, minced

1 tablespoon capers

Sea salt and freshly ground black pepper to taste

8 ounces mâche or butter lettuce, torn into bite-size pieces (about 5 cups)

Mix all of the ingredients except the mâche thoroughly in a large mixing bowl. Put the mâche leaves on a large serving platter and spoon the salad over the top. Serve immediately.

The best tool to have for this salad is an inexpensive slicer that's available in many Asian markets. It's the easiest and safest way to "shave" the fennel paper thin without scraping or slicing your thumbs. (It also works for the Parmesan cheese.) When the fennel is thinly sliced, the flavor is very delicate, and it absorbs the dressing much more quickly.   **Serves 4 to 6**

Fennel Salad with Mozzarella and Tomatoes

1 large fennel bulb, halved and sliced as thinly as possible (white part only)

1 cup plum tomatoes, cut into thin slivers (about 6 ounces)

2/3 cup minced green onions (white and green parts)

1 cup shredded fresh mozzarella cheese (about 4 ounces)

1/3 cup kalamata olives

2 1/2 tablespoons fresh lemon juice

2 teaspoons lemon zest

Sea salt and freshly ground black pepper to taste

1 head butter lettuce, torn into bite-size pieces

1/3 cup very thinly sliced or shaved Parmesan cheese

Minced fennel fronds for garnish (optional)

2 tablespoons extra-virgin olive oil

1. Mix together the fennel slices, tomato slivers, green onions, mozzarella, and olives in a large bowl. Stir in the lemon juice and lemon zest and season the salad with salt and pepper.

2. Place the lettuce on a large serving plate and spoon the fennel salad over the top. Decorate with the Parmesan cheese and any minced fennel fronds, if desired. Just before serving, drizzle the olive oil over the top.

For this salad, be sure to use whole cherry tomatoes. With their skin intact, the liquid from the grapefruit won't penetrate the tomatoes and make them watery. Peel the whole grapefruits with a knife, removing the white pith. Then, with a small paring knife, section the fruit in between each of the membranes. The result will be a beautiful, clean, and elegant salad.

Serves 4

Ruby Grapefruit, Tomato, and Mozzarella Salad

2 large ripe pink grapefruits, peels removed and sectioned

1 cup whole cherry tomatoes

2 heads red Belgian endive or regular endive

12 bocconcini mozzarella balls (about 1½ pounds)

1 tablespoon minced fresh chives

1 teaspoon sea salt

½ teaspoon freshly ground black pepper

1 tablespoon olive oil

1. Place the grapefruit sections and tomatoes in a medium-size serving bowl. Slice the endive heads in half lengthwise. Cut them into julienne strips and add to the bowl, along with the cheese.

2. Stir in the chives, salt, and pepper and drizzle the oil over the top. Stir the salad gently, cover with plastic wrap, and refrigerate for 30 minutes or up to 1 day. Just before serving, sprinkle the top with additional freshly ground pepper, if desired. Serve the salad slightly chilled.

Here's a tangy version of the classic salad, designed for eating with just a fork. Feel free to 'make this up to several days in advance, because it just gets better and better as the flavors meld. If you do that, though, wait until 30 minutes before serving to add the cheese.

Serves 4 to 6

Caprese Chopped Salad

½ pound ripe yellow cherry tomatoes, quartered

½ pound red cherry tomatoes, quartered

1 small sweet red onion, minced

1 small red bell pepper, diced

½ small cucumber, peeled, seeded, and diced

½ cup diced cornichons (French-style pickles)

3 tablespoons Dijon mustard

2 tablespoons minced fresh tarragon

½ cup minced fresh Italian parsley

¼ cup capers, chopped

2 tablespoons red wine vinegar

¾ cup extra-virgin olive oil

8 ounces fresh mozzarella cheese

2 cups mâche or arugula leaves

1. In a large bowl, mix together the tomatoes, onion, bell pepper, cucumber, and cornichons. In a medium-size bowl, whisk the mustard, herbs, capers, and vinegar. Whisk in the oil and add to the vegetables.

2. Cut half of the mozzarella into ¼-inch cubes and gently fold into the salad. Slice the remaining mozzarella into thin rounds.

3. Line a serving bowl with the mâche. Place the rounds of cheese on top of the greens and spoon the vegetable mixture over the top. Allow the salad to marinate for 30 minutes before serving.

Classic Caprese Salad

A perfect, classic Caprese salad is as easy as can be to prepare. Start with the freshest, juiciest tomatoes you can find, and slice them into rounds. Slice a very fresh ball of mozzarella cheese into rounds, and layer the two in an overlapping pattern on a platter. Tuck fresh Italian basil leaves in between the tomatoes and mozzarella slices, and drizzle top-quality extra-virgin olive oil over the top. Lightly sprinkle everything with a little sea salt. Serve the *insalata Caprese* immediately, at room temperature, along with a chilled bottle of Italian white wine and some artisan Italian bread.

Classic olive tapenade served as the inspiration for this tangy, rich variation on the theme. The mozzarella tames the strong sun-dried tomato flavor. As a quick appetizer, instead of using the tapenade in a salad, as we do here, spread the tapenade on crispy croutons or crackers. Store leftover tapenade in the refrigerator for up to two weeks, and use it to top grilled chicken or fish, or as a delicious sandwich spread. Toast the pine nuts in a single layer in a 350°F oven for about 10 minutes.   **Serves 4 to 6**

Summer Salad of Tomato and Mozzarella Tapenade

1   1-pound ball fresh mozzarella cheese

1   8-ounce jar sun-dried tomatoes in olive oil

¼   cup pine nuts, toasted

⅓   cup chopped fresh Italian parsley

⅓   cup finely grated Parmesan cheese

2   medium-size garlic cloves, chopped

1   head butter lettuce, separated into leaves

2   medium-size ripe beefsteak tomatoes, each thickly sliced into 4 rounds

Extra-virgin olive oil

1. Cut the mozzarella ball into quarters. Cut 3 of the quarters into 1-inch cubes and the remaining quarter into 8 slices. Place the cubed mozzarella, sun-dried tomatoes, pine nuts, parsley, Parmesan cheese, and garlic in a food processor and pulse until slightly chunky.

2. Line a large serving platter with the lettuce leaves. Spread each tomato slice and mozzarella slice with 1 heaping tablespoon of the sun-dried tomato tapenade and place them on the lettuce. Lightly drizzle the olive oil over the salad. Serve immediately, or cover and refrigerate for up to 4 hours. Bring to room temperature before serving.

At the end of Rue Rosier in the Marais district of Paris is a hidden treasure called Loir dans la Thèiére, or Door Mouse in the Teapot. A charming French tearoom with walls covered in *Alice's Adventures in Wonderland* memorabilia, the Thèiére serves some of the best casual lunches in town. This sublime dish, their take on the classic Caprese, is part of its summer salad offerings and is usually served with eggplant caviar, roasted red peppers, and very crusty fresh bread. Because this is a simple dish, the small effort it takes to peel the tomatoes makes a big difference in this case, as does using *fleur de sel,* a French salt from the Camargue.

Serves 4

The Teapot's Tomatoes

4 medium-size orange or red heirloom tomatoes, cored

4 ounces fresh mozzarella cheese, cut into thick slabs

½ teaspoon *fleur de sel* or sea salt

1 tablespoon store-bought basil-flavored olive oil

4 basil leaves

1. Carve a small ✕ on the bottom of each tomato. Fill a sink or large bowl with cold water. Bring a large pot of salted water to a boil and add the tomatoes. Remove them after about 30 seconds, or when the skins just begin to blister, and place them in the cold water.

2. Drain and peel the tomatoes. Place them in a colander core-side down. Set aside for a half hour.

3. Place the cheese on a large platter and top with the tomatoes. Sprinkle them very lightly with salt and drizzle with the oil. Top each one with a basil leaf.

The first really flavorful tomatoes usually show up at the market when asparagus is still in season. This salad is a perfect way to celebrate both, especially if you can find the large Yellow Perfection heirloom tomatoes. If you can't find white asparagus, the regular green kind works just fine. You can make the whole platter and dressing several hours ahead and spoon the dressing on just before serving. You'll know summer's here!   **Serves 4**

Red and Yellow Tomatoes with Mozzarella and White Asparagus

For the vinaigrette

1   large ripe red tomato, cored and halved

2   tablespoons store-bought prepared sun-dried tomato pesto

2   tablespoons fresh lemon juice

Zest of 1 lemon

¼   cup extra-virgin olive oil

1   tablespoon minced fresh basil

Sea salt and freshly ground black pepper to taste

1   pound white asparagus, ends peeled

1   large ripe red tomato, cored and cut into eighths

1   large yellow tomato, cored and cut into eighths

8   bocconcini mozzarella balls

1. To make the vinaigrette, place a box grater over a bowl and grate the tomato halves, with the cut sides against the grater. Discard the skin. Whisk in the pesto, lemon juice, and lemon zest. Slowly whisk in the oil. Add the basil and season to taste with salt and pepper.

2. To make the asparagus, bring the water to a boil in an asparagus or vegetable steamer and steam the asparagus just until tender, 5 to 7 minutes. Remove from the steamer and let cool slightly. Line a serving platter with the asparagus and surround it with the tomatoes and cheese. Spoon the dressing over the platter and serve immediately.

We first tasted this salad at La Scala in Buis-les-Barrionnes, a small village bistro in the Rhone Valley. The sweet and very delicate tomato sauce was made with tiny ripe tomatoes and was a sensuous foil for the cheese and salty olives. If you've ever thought of visiting Provence, or even if you know it well, make this salad and you're halfway there!   **Serves 4**

Warm and Cool Tomato Salad

For the tomato sauce

2	tablespoons extra-virgin olive oil
1	garlic clove, minced
1	shallot, minced
1	pound small ripe red plum tomatoes, quartered
	Sea salt and freshly ground black pepper to taste

For the salad

1	medium-size ripe red tomato, cored and cut into 4 thick slices
4	slices day-old country bread, sliced 1 inch thick and trimmed into rounds
3	tablespoons extra-virgin olive oil
1	tablespoon balsamic vinegar
2	teaspoons *herbes de Provence*
4	¼-inch-thick rounds fresh mozzarella cheese, shaped to fit the bread rounds
½	head romaine lettuce, shredded or cut into thin strips
½	medium-size cucumber, thinly sliced, for garnish
	Cured olives, for garnish

1. To make the sauce, in a medium-size skillet, heat the olive oil over medium heat and sauté the garlic and shallot for 1 minute, or until softened. Add the tomatoes, salt, and pepper and cook over medium-low heat until the tomatoes are slightly softened, about 10 minutes. The tomato juice will have evaporated and the tomatoes will have a creamy appearance.

2. Preheat the oven to 400°F.

3. To make the salad, place the tomato slices on the bread rounds. Make the dressing by whisking together the olive oil, vinegar, *herbes de Provence*, salt, and pepper. Brush a little over the tomatoes and top with cheese. Bake until the cheese is just melted, 7 to 10 minutes.

4. Spoon the warm tomato sauce onto a large serving platter. Toss the lettuce with the remaining vinaigrette and place over the tomato sauce. Arrange the bread rounds on top of the lettuce and arrange the cucumber rounds and olives around the edges of the platter. Serve immediately.

Panzanella, that clever Italian salad that uses summer vegetables to dress up stale bread, can be rather dry and boring. Thanks to my dear friend Jay London, a creative cook with a discerning palate, this tomato panzanella is full of flavor, moist, and well balanced. It's Jay's dressing that puts it over the edge. The olive tapenade, lemon, and hint of cayenne are a stroke of culinary genius.

Serves 4 to 6

Tomato Panzanella with Mozzarella and Olivada

1	medium-size red onion, halved and thinly sliced
2/3	cup minced green onions (white and green parts)
1/2	medium-size English cucumber, diced
1	tablespoon capers
3	medium-size ripe tomatoes, cored and coarsely chopped
1	large garlic clove, minced
8	ounces day-old focaccia or hearty Italian bread
1/4	cup lemon basil or regular basil leaves, coarsely chopped
1	cup shredded mozzarella cheese
	Olivada Dressing (at right)

Place all the ingredients in a large bowl and gently toss to mix well. Serve immediately, or cover and refrigerate for up to 1 day, but allow to come to room temperature before serving.

Olivada Dressing

Makes about 1/3 cup

2 tablespoons store-bought olive tapenade
1 tablespoon fresh lemon juice
1/4 cup extra-virgin olive oil
1 garlic clove, minced
Pinch of cayenne pepper

Whisk all the ingredients together in a small bowl. Store in the refrigerator in a clean glass container for up to 3 days.

We first developed a version of this recipe several years ago, when Hallie was the executive chef of the Nicollet Island Inn in Minneapolis, Minnesota. The inn was pioneering, with one of the first restaurants devoted to promoting Midwestern delicacies such as wild rice and local herbs. As a feature on the inn's "Minnesota Made" menus, the dish was a hit for years. It's easy to make any time of the year and adapts beautifully to any edible wild mushroom.

Serves 4

Wild Mushroom, Wild Rice, Tomato, and Mozzarella Salad

⅓ cup wild rice

3 cups water

4 ounces trumpet mushrooms

6 ounces portobello mushrooms

3 tablespoons olive oil

2 large garlic cloves

½ cup homemade or store-bought chicken broth

1 cup halved cherry tomatoes (about 5 ounces)

Sea salt and freshly ground black pepper to taste

Pinch of cayenne pepper

½ cup tightly packed julienned fresh basil leaves

1 cup shredded mozzarella cheese

4 ounces mâche lettuce, torn into bite-size pieces

1. Place the rice and water in a medium-size saucepan. Lightly salt the water and bring it to a boil, uncovered. Cover and boil over medium-low heat for 40 minutes, or until the rice is tender. Drain the rice and set it aside to cool.

2. Remove the stems from both types of mushrooms. Slice the trumpet mushrooms lengthwise into quarters. Cut the portobellos into ¼-inch-thick slices.

3. Heat the olive oil in a large skillet over medium-high heat. Add the garlic cloves and sauté for 3 minutes. Remove the garlic and discard it. The oil will be smoking hot. Immediately add all the mushrooms and sauté for 3 minutes, or until all the oil is absorbed. Pour in the broth and cook until the broth is absorbed, about 1 minute. Stir in the tomatoes and cook for 1 minute. Season with salt, black pepper, and cayenne pepper. Remove the mixture from the heat and stir in the basil. Stir until the basil has wilted, then let the mixture cool slightly.

4. Stir the mozzarella into the rice. Line a serving platter or shallow bowl with the mâche. Place the rice mixture in the bowl and top with the mushrooms. Stir gently to mix the salad and serve.

Here's an easy and filling vegetarian lunch. You will want a bowl of mixed greens, a pitcher of chilled cider, and a loaf of bread to round it out. Use quick-cooking barley to cut down the preparation time even more. You can make this up to a day ahead; just remove it from the refrigerator at least 45 minutes before serving.   **Serves 4 to 6**

Spring Barley Salad

½ cup pearl barley

2½ cups water

1 teaspoon salt

3 cups chopped ripe tomatoes

2 celery stalks, chopped

½ medium-size white onion, diced

2 cups ½-inch fresh mozzarella cheese cubes (8 ounces)

2 tablespoons tightly packed minced fresh Italian parsley

2 tablespoons fresh lemon juice

2 tablespoons extra-virgin olive oil

Pinch of cayenne pepper

Sea salt and freshly ground black pepper to taste

1. Place the barley, water, and salt in a large saucepan and bring to a boil. Cover and cook over medium heat for 30 minutes, or until tender. Drain the barley and place it in a large bowl.

2. Add the tomatoes, celery, onion, mozzarella cubes, and parsley. Stir in the lemon juice and olive oil. Add the cayenne pepper and season to taste with salt and black pepper. Mix to combine, and serve at room temperature.

This refreshing room-temperature salad is a snap if you buy the preseasoned tabbouleh mixture that is sold in bulk at many whole-foods and health food stores. The crispy "chips" are fun with this salad and also make a good garnish for almost any green salad or appetizer platter. Unlike their famous cousins, Parmesan chips, these are chewier and should be served the day you make them.

Serves 6

Tomato Tabbouleh Salad with Crispy Mozzarella Chips

1¾ cups dry store-bought seasoned tabbouleh

1½ cups boiling water

2 large ripe beefsteak tomatoes, chopped

2 cups shredded mozzarella cheese

2 tablespoons minced fresh cilantro leaves

½ cup minced green onions (white and green parts)

1 medium-size zucchini, diced

1 tablespoon olive oil

2 tablespoons fresh lemon juice

Sea salt and freshly ground black pepper to taste

1. Preheat the oven to 350°F.

2. Place the tabbouleh in a large bowl. Add the water and cover. Steep the tabbouleh for 5 minutes, or until all of the water has been absorbed. Mix in the tomatoes, 1 cup of the mozzarella, the cilantro, green onions, zucchini, olive oil, and lemon juice. Season lightly with salt and pepper, and set aside.

3. Place tablespoonfuls of the remaining 1 cup mozzarella in small mounds on a parchment paper–lined baking sheet. Bake for 7 to 10 minutes, or until the outside edges are golden brown and the cheese has melted together. Remove from the baking sheet and place the chips on paper towels.

4. Put the tabbouleh in a large serving bowl and serve with the chips.

Café Max, a classic Parisian bistro, serves its classic lentil salad with a sharp, mustardy vinaigrette. Max was an inspiration for this lighter, creamier version. When making the salad, feel free to experiment with different colors of both domestic and imported lentils and tomatoes. Serve with a basket of warm bread and a round of bone-dry white wine.   **Serves 2**

Tomato Lentil Salad

1   cup green lentils

4   cups water

1   teaspoon dried thyme

2   small bay leaves

2   garlic cloves, peeled

½   medium-size white onion, quartered

2   teaspoons sea salt

3   cups diced ripe red tomatoes (about 1 pound)

1   tablespoon store-bought prepared basil pesto

1   cup shredded mozzarella cheese

1. Place the lentils in a medium-size saucepan over high heat and add the water. Add the thyme, bay leaves, garlic cloves, and onion. Bring the mixture to a boil, cover, and reduce the heat to a simmer. Cook for 30 minutes, or until the lentils are tender. Some brands of lentils may require more water, so check the pot after 15 minutes and add more if all the liquid has been absorbed.

2. When the lentils are cooked, remove them from the heat and drain any excess liquid. Discard the bay leaves. Add the salt, tomatoes, pesto, and ½ cup of the cheese. Set aside for 15 minutes. Just before serving, taste the salad and add additional salt, if desired. Sprinkle the remaining ½ cup of cheese over the top and serve, or cover and refrigerate for up to 1 day.

The secret to this fork-tender chicken breast is to sauté a few humble vegetables before adding the chicken and the liquid. The result is perfectly cooked chicken that is the perfect foil for the thick tomato dressing. By the way, there is a hidden bonus here. Although the dressing is rich and packed with flavor, it is extremely low in fat and calories since no oil is used. Enjoy!   Serves 4

Chicken Salad with Cheesy Tomato-Basil Dressing

3   large ripe red tomatoes

⅓   cup cottage cheese

2   cups chopped fresh mozzarella cheese (about 10 ounces)

1   tablespoon balsamic vinegar

2   tightly packed tablespoons chopped fresh basil leaves

    Sea salt and freshly ground black pepper

1   tablespoon olive oil

½   large yellow onion, finely chopped

1   medium-size carrot, finely chopped

1   celery stalk, finely chopped

1¼ pounds boneless chicken breasts

2   cups homemade or store-bought chicken or vegetable broth

1   small head of romaine lettuce, julienned

½   English cucumber, very thinly sliced

2   tablespoons freshly minced chives

1. Chop 2 of the tomatoes and place them in a blender. Dice the remaining tomato and set it aside. Add the cottage cheese, ½ cup of the mozzarella cheese, and the vinegar to the blender and blend until liquefied and smooth. Remove from the blender and stir in the basil leaves. Season to taste with salt and pepper. Set the dressing aside, or cover and refrigerate for up to 2 days.

2. Heat the oil in a large skillet and sauté the onion, carrot, and celery over medium heat for 2 minutes. Place the chicken breasts on top of the vegetables and pour the broth around the sides of the skillet. Cover and cook for 15 minutes. Remove from the heat and let the chicken cool in the broth, covered.

3. Thinly slice the meat on the diagonal. Line a serving platter with the lettuce and arrange the chicken over the greens. Scatter the remaining mozzarella around the platter, along with the cucumber slices. Sprinkle the dish with the chives and reserved diced tomato. Serve the tomato dressing on the side in a small pitcher or bottle. If the dressing has been made ahead and seems too thick, you may thin it with a little of the chicken poaching liquid.

A clear serving bowl is the key to winning a visual award with this easy salad. If you make this ahead of time, it will taste even better, as the flavors will have a chance to develop. If time allows, brush some garlic-flavored olive oil over cut-up day-old tortillas and bake them until they are crispy. They create a wonderful garnish.

Serves 6

Southwestern Layered Black Bean Salad with Smoked Mozzarella

1 ancho chile

4 ounces smoked bacon

2 garlic cloves, minced

1 medium-size white onion, chopped

Sea salt and freshly ground black pepper

½ teaspoon ground cumin

1 15-ounce can black beans, rinsed and drained

3 tablespoons fresh lime juice

3 tablespoons finely minced cilantro

2 cups frozen corn kernels, defrosted

½ cup finely chopped green onions (white and green parts)

1 large red bell pepper, diced

1 pound plum tomatoes, halved

4 cups shredded smoked mozzarella cheese (about 1 pound)

2 tablespoons Tomato-Chili Oil (page 158), plus more for serving

2 additional limes, cut into small wedges, for garnish

1. Soak the ancho chile in very warm water until softened, about 25 minutes. Drain and cut into ⅛-inch slivers. Set aside.

2. Heat a large skillet over medium heat and fry the bacon slices until crisp. Remove them from the pan and drain on paper towels. Crumble the bacon and set aside.

3. Reheat the skillet over medium heat without wiping out the accumulated fat. Sauté the chile, garlic, and onion. Season with salt and pepper as the mixture cooks. Stir in the cumin and cook for 30 seconds. Add the beans and cook for 30 seconds, stirring to thoroughly mix the ingredients. Remove from the heat and add 2 tablespoons of the lime juice, the crumbled bacon, and 2 tablespoons of the cilantro. Mix and set aside to cool.

4. Place the corn in a small bowl and stir in the remaining 1 tablespoon lime juice and 1 tablespoon cilantro. Season the corn with salt and pepper and mix.

5. Place 1 cup of the beans in the bottom of a clear serving bowl. Sprinkle ¼ cup of the green onions over the beans. Top with half of the red pepper, followed by 1 cup of the corn and half of the tomatoes. Top this with half of the mozzarella. Repeat the layering, using the remaining ingredients. Drizzle the tomato-chili oil over the top. Cover and refrigerate for at least 2 hours before serving, or up to 1 day. Serve at room temperature accompanied by the lime wedges and additional tomato-chili oil.

Savory Soups
and Sandwiches

A little saffron goes a long way. Just a few threads in this chilled soup give an exotic, haunting taste that is addictive. Pass a large bowl of croutons to float in the soup. If you're lucky enough to have any leftovers, they will freeze beautifully. So when the garden is producing tomatoes like mad, make a big batch of this to have on hand whenever you crave it. You can also prepare this a day ahead, making it great for entertaining. **Serves 6 to 8**

Dazzling Tomato Soup with Mozzarella

2 tablespoons olive oil

1 medium-size red onion, diced

Sea salt and freshly ground black pepper to taste

3 pounds ripe tomatoes, peeled and crushed, with their seeds

2 cloves garlic, thinly sliced

2 large sprigs fresh thyme, leaves only

½ cup red wine

1½ cups water

¼ teaspoon saffron threads

1 cup plain yogurt (low-fat okay)

For the garnish

1 large ripe yellow or red tomato, diced

½ cup diced fresh mozzarella cheese (about 2 ounces)

½ cup sour cream

1. Heat the olive oil over medium heat in a large saucepan or stockpot. Add the onion and season with salt and pepper. Sauté for 5 minutes or until the onion has softened. Add the tomatoes, garlic, thyme, red wine, water, and saffron. Heat to a simmer and cook over low heat for 20 minutes. Remove from the heat and allow to cool.

2. Blend the soup in a food processor or blender until it is almost smooth. (A few chunks are fine.) Place the soup in a large bowl and whisk in the yogurt. Cover and chill the soup in the refrigerator for at least 4 hours or overnight.

3. When ready to serve, make the garnish by mixing together the diced tomato and mozzarella in a small bowl. Whisk the sour cream in another small bowl to soften it. Ladle the soup into bowls and top each with a spoonful of sour cream and a small spoonful of the tomato-cheese mixture.

Although we like to serve this Italian chilled soup as a first course, this is certainly substantial enough for a main course on a hot summer day. Serve with a big bowl of summer fruits and a tray of biscotti and you've got a winning lunch for friends.

Serves 6 to 8

Summer Tomato Risotto Soup

5 cups diced ripe medium-size plum tomatoes (about 1½ pounds)

1 medium-size red onion, thinly sliced

1 large English cucumber, diced

1 cup shredded mozzarella cheese

½ cup diced store-bought roasted red peppers

4 cups homemade or store-bought chicken or vegetable broth

2 tablespoons store-bought basil or hot pepper oil

Few drops of red wine vinegar

Sea salt and freshly ground black pepper to taste

1 large bunch fresh basil, stemmed, and leaves torn into bite-size pieces

24 bocconcini or ciliegine mozzarella balls

For the rice

1 cup Arborio rice

3 cups homemade or store-bought chicken broth

½ teaspoon sea salt

1. To make the rice, place the rice, broth, and salt in a medium-size saucepan and bring to a boil. Reduce the heat to a simmer, cover the pan, and cook for 20 minutes. Turn off the heat and let the rice stand for 5 minutes to cook further. Remove the cover and let the rice cool slightly.

2. Place the tomatoes, onion, cucumber, shredded mozzarella, peppers, cooked rice, and broth in a large bowl. Season the mixture with the basil oil, vinegar, salt, and pepper. Cover and chill the soup for at least 2 hours and up to 3 days. If the rice has absorbed most of the liquid, add additional broth to thin it to a thick, soupy consistency.

3. Just before serving, slice the basil leaves into long shreds. Ladle the soup into bowls and garnish each bowl with the basil and 3 bocconcini balls. Serve immediately.

Here's our twist on the classic Spanish soup. The different colors of ripe tomatoes, refreshing mint, and soft cheese garnish make this gazpacho a real hit. Every tomato is different, so tasting is the key here. Some will need a little more salt, more vinegar, or, in some cases, even a pinch of sugar. Make this up to a day ahead and serve it as a first course or a lunch along with hunks of grilled hearty bread and a cruet of good-quality olive oil for drizzling.   **Serves 4**

Tricolored Gazpacho

2 each ripe red, orange, and yellow tomatoes (about 2 pounds total), cored and cut into sixths

1 large garlic clove

1 medium-size red onion, cut into eighths

2 small purple or green bell peppers, seeded and coarsely chopped

1 English cucumber, coarsely chopped

2 tablespoons fresh mint leaves, plus a handful for garnish

Sea salt to taste

Sherry vinegar to taste

Pinch of cayenne pepper

½ cup quartered cherry tomatoes

¾ cup diced fresh mozzarella cheese (about 3 ounces)

2 ½-inch-thick French bread slices, cut in ¼-inch cubes

1 tablespoon olive oil

1. Place the tomatoes, garlic, onion, all but ½ cup of the peppers, all but ½ cup of the cucumber, and the mint in a blender and puree into a slightly chunky texture. (This most likely must be done in batches.) Remove the soup to a large serving bowl. Taste and season with salt, vinegar, and cayenne pepper as desired. Cover the soup and refrigerate until well chilled. Taste again and reseason, if necessary.

2. Mince the remaining ½ cup chopped peppers and ½ cup cucumber and place side by side on a serving platter. Place the cherry tomatoes and cheese side by side on the platter. In a small skillet, sauté the bread cubes in the oil until golden. Drain and place on the platter. Scatter the entire platter with a few additional mint leaves. Serve the gazpacho in individual bowls, passing the serving platter of garnishes at the table.

Traditionally, this thick Florentine soup is flavored with sage. However, we found that the fennel seed flavor blended beautifully with the basil pesto, so we omitted the sage for this version. We also used canned organic fire-roasted tomatoes, which make this soup doable all year round. In the summer, serve it at room temperature, and on a blustery February evening, serve it piping hot. Either way, it's comforting, filling, and delicious. **Serves 8**

Pappa al Pomodoro

2	teaspoons fennel seeds
3	tablespoons olive oil
1	shallot, minced
2	garlic cloves, minced
8	ounces day-old hearty French-style sourdough bread, thinly sliced
1	28-ounce can plus one 14.5-ounce can fire-roasted diced tomatoes
1	cup white wine
1	cup water
	Sea salt and freshly ground black pepper to taste
2	tablespoons store-bought prepared basil pesto
2	cups shredded mozzarella cheese
1/2	cup grated Parmesan cheese

1. Lightly crush the fennel seeds with a mortar and pestle or in a spice grinder.

2. Heat the olive oil in a large saucepan over medium heat. Sauté the shallot and garlic for 3 minutes, until the garlic is lightly colored. Add the bread slices and sauté for about 5 minutes, stirring frequently, until the bread is also lightly colored and crumbled.

3. Stir in the tomatoes, wine, and water. Season lightly with salt and pepper. Simmer, uncovered, for 25 to 30 minutes, or until the soup is very thick. Stir in the pesto and remove from the heat.

4. Spoon into bowls and top each bowl with 1/4 cup of the mozzarella and 1 tablespoon of the Parmesan. Serve immediately.

This soup was inspired by author Mary Evans, who often blends regional American dishes like chowder with Mediterranean ingredients. In this case, we have created the perfect melting pot. Traditional potato chowder is enhanced with not only Italian garbanzo beans and red wine, but also our beloved tomatoes and mozzarella. If you believe it can't be chowder without milk, call it what you like, but it's still delicious. Bravo, Mary, for this tasty combination!

Serves 4

Tomato Chickpea Chowder

2 tablespoons olive oil

1 large onion, chopped

1 15-ounce can chickpeas, drained and rinsed

2 large garlic cloves, minced

1½ teaspoons chopped fresh rosemary

1 14.5-ounce can diced tomatoes, with their juice

1 14-ounce can reduced-sodium chicken broth

2 medium-size red boiling potatoes, cut into ½-inch pieces

½ cup red wine

Pinch of red pepper flakes

⅛ teaspoon freshly ground black pepper

¾ cup shredded mozzarella cheese

1. Heat the olive oil in a Dutch oven or heavy soup pot over medium heat. Add the onion and sauté until softened, 4 to 5 minutes. Stir in the chickpeas, garlic, and rosemary and sauté until aromatic, about 1 minute. Remove from the heat. Reserve 1 cup of the mixture. Add the tomatoes and their juice to the pot, along with the chicken broth.

2. Puree the mixture using an immersion blender, or puree it in batches using a blender or food processor, and return it to the pot. Stir in the potatoes, red wine, and red pepper flakes. Bring to a boil over medium heat, then reduce the heat to medium-low. Gently boil, uncovered, stirring occasionally, until the potatoes are just tender, about 20 minutes. Stir in the reserved chickpea mixture and the black pepper. Reheat to a simmer and ladle into 4 soup bowls. Sprinkle with the shredded mozzarella and serve.

These simple and satisfying sandwiches are wonderful for picnics, as they can be assembled and wrapped in foil several hours ahead and then grilled later on. Make sure to purchase very fresh pita bread so that you can easily split them in half when stuffing them. You will have leftover sun-dried tomato paste, so try it tossed with pasta on another day.   **Serves 4**

Picnic Pitas

Sun-Dried Tomato Paste

½ cup sun-dried tomatoes packed in oil

¼ cup olive oil

1 large garlic clove, peeled

1 teaspoon dried Italian seasoning

1 tablespoon fresh lemon juice

Zest of 1 lemon

Pinch of sea salt and cayenne pepper

4 large pita breads, halved

1½ cups chopped ripe tomatoes (about ½ pound)

1 cup shredded mozzarella cheese

1. Prepare a hot fire in a grill.

2. Place all of the sun-dried tomato paste ingredients in the bowl of a food processor and mix into a soft paste.

3. Spread 1 generous tablespoon sun-dried tomato paste over the insides of each pita half. Divide the chopped tomatoes and shredded cheese equally between the pita halves. Wrap each half in foil. Grill over a medium flame for 6 to 8 minutes. Serve warm or at room temperature.

For this sandwich, you will bake rosy-colored long bread loaves infused with tomato and roasted pepper flavor, then slice them and top with fresh tomatoes and mozzarella. Serve these sandwiches open face, with a knife and a fork alongside.

Serves 6 to 8

Blushing Baguettes

½ cup coarsely chopped store-bought roasted red bell peppers

2 tablespoons tomato paste

1 tablespoon sugar

1 teaspoon sweet paprika

¾ cup warm water

1½ tablespoons dry yeast

½ cup polenta or coarse cornmeal

1½ teaspoons salt

½ cup finely chopped green onions (white and green parts)

2 tablespoons olive oil

4½ cups white bread flour

3 tablespoons store-bought basil oil

8 ounces fresh mozzarella cheese, cut into ¼-inch-thick slices

2 large beefsteak tomatoes, thinly sliced

2 tightly packed tablespoons chopped fresh basil leaves

1. Puree the peppers, tomato paste, sugar, paprika, and water in a food processor or blender. Sprinkle the yeast over the top and pulse to mix. Let the mixture sit for about 5 minutes, then pour it into a large mixing bowl. Add the polenta, salt, green onions, and olive oil.

2. Mix in about 2½ cups of the flour and blend until it forms a shaggy mass. Then turn the dough out onto a floured surface and knead, adding additional flour as needed to prevent the dough from sticking, for 10 minutes, or until it is soft and elastic. Place it in an oiled bowl and let it rise, covered, for 1 hour, or until the dough has doubled in size.

3. Gently deflate the dough and knead for 1 minute. Shape it into two 10-inch-long baguettes and place them on an oiled parchment paper–lined baking sheet. Cover and let rise for 1 hour.

4. Preheat the oven to 375°F.

5. Make three ¼-inch slashes on top of each baguette. Bake the baguettes for 25 minutes, or until golden brown. Remove from the oven and place the loaves on a cooling rack. Allow them to cool completely before slicing.

6. To assemble the sandwiches, slice the baguettes into ½-inch-thick rounds and brush with basil oil. Top each round with a slice each of cheese and tomato, brush with a little more oil, and top with a generous pinch of basil. Serve immediately.

Traditionally, brioche are small individual egg buns with cute little knobs on top. However, the dough makes a great loaf bread as well, as seen in these buttery, salty, open-face Mediterranean sandwiches. The brioche recipe makes two loaves, but you need only one loaf for the sandwiches, so by all means freeze the other loaf to have on hand. Note that you must refrigerate the dough overnight before baking the bread.

Serves 8

Olive Brioche with Grilled Eggplant, Mozzarella, and Tomatoes

⅓ cup milk, slightly warmed

1 tablespoon active dry yeast

⅓ cup sugar

3½ cups all-purpose flour

6 large eggs

1½ teaspoons sea salt

½ cup (1 stick) unsalted butter, softened

½ cup store-bought olive tapenade

1 large globe eggplant, sliced into ¼-inch rounds

3 tablespoons store-bought basil oil

1 pound fresh mozzarella cheese, cut into ¼-inch rounds

3 large ripe beefsteak tomatoes, cut into ¼-inch rounds

1. Place the milk in the bowl of an electric mixer and stir in the yeast and a pinch of the sugar until dissolved. Let the mixture proof for 5 minutes.

2. Stir in 1 cup of the flour. Lightly beat 1 egg and stir it into the dough. Sprinkle 1 cup additional flour over the top and let rise, uncovered, for 30 minutes.

3. Using the dough hook on slow speed, add the remaining sugar, the salt, 4 lightly beaten eggs, and 1 more cup of the flour. Mix the dough into a sticky mass, then add the remaining ½ cup flour. Increase the mixer speed to medium and beat for 10 minutes. Add the butter, 2 tablespoons at a time, then beat in ¼ cup of the tapenade. The dough will be very sticky. Cover the bowl and let the dough rise for 1 hour, then refrigerate overnight.

4. Remove the dough and let it sit at room temperature for 20 minutes. Preheat the oven to 375°F.

5. Butter two 9-inch loaf pans and scrape the sticky dough into the pans. Let the brioche dough rise in the pans for 2 to 2½ hours, or until it has doubled in bulk. Beat the remaining egg with 1 tablespoon water and

(continued)

Olive Brioche with Grilled Eggplant, Mozzarella, and Tomatoes

(continued)

brush it over the surface of the dough. Slash the top of each loaf in 3 places. Bake on the middle shelf for 35 to 40 minutes, or until golden brown. Remove and allow the brioche to cool on a cooling rack.

6. Prepare a hot fire in a grill.

7. Brush the eggplant with the basil oil and grill until browned and softened. Remove and spread each slice with a generous teaspoon of tapenade. Set the eggplant aside.

8. Remove the brioche from the pans and cut 1 loaf into 8 slices. Lightly grill the brioche slices and place them on a large serving platter. Top with the warm eggplant, 1 or 2 slices of cheese, and the sliced tomato. Any leftover tapenade can be used to garnish the tops. Serve immediately.

Got kids? Sitting around a campfire or a backyard grill? Here's a "sandwich" that will be fun to make and will please the parents as much as the youngsters! Alternatively, it is also a surprisingly sophisticated appetizer for even those guests with been-there, done-that palates. In other words, you can win everyone's heart, young or old, with the ultimate grilled cheese.

Serves 8

Open-Face Grilled Cheese Sandwiches

8 thin slices fresh baguette, sliced on the diagonal

½ cup mayonnaise

2 tablespoons store-bought prepared basil pesto

1 large ripe beefsteak tomato, cut into 8 slices

4 ovalini mozzarella balls (about 1 pound), cut in half

8 large basil leaves

1. Prepare a hot fire in a grill. Toast the bread on both sides until slightly crisp.

2. In a small bowl, mix together the mayonnaise and pesto. Spread 1 tablespoon on each slice of toast. Top each slice with a tomato slice. Place the prepared toasts on a large platter near the grill.

3. Skewer the ovalini halves onto 8 metal skewers and hold each skewer over the fire until the cheese begins to melt. (This may take 2 people and is best done in batches.) When the cheese starts melting, scrape it off onto the prepared toasts, top each with a basil leaf, and serve immediately.

This typical niçoise street food is really a French hero sandwich. Serve it with plenty of napkins, as this delicious combo will more than likely dribble down your chin. In France, it's usually served in waxed paper, which collects all the oil and manages to get it all over whatever else you've bought! To play it safe, sit down and eat this with a knife and fork. The weighting of the pan bagnat is crucial! The bread soaks up all of the flavors from the filling and really turns this into a "hero" of a sandwich.   **Serves 4**

Tomato Pan Bagnat

2	large garlic cloves, minced
3	tablespoons olive oil
4	large crusty French bread rolls, halved
1	6-ounce can water-packed tuna
1	tablespoon capers
1	large ripe tomato, cored and sliced ¼ inch thick
1	6-ounce jar marinated artichokes, quartered
4	ounces fresh mozzarella cheese, thinly sliced
1	large green onion, halved and thinly sliced
½	cup thinly sliced store-bought roasted red peppers

1. Mix together the garlic and olive oil in a small bowl. Spread the mixture over the cut sides of the rolls. Add the tuna and capers to the bowl, mix well, and spread a layer on half of each roll. Top the tuna with a tomato slice, a piece of artichoke, a slice of cheese, and some green onion. Top with a few pepper strips. Place the other half of the roll over the peppers and press down to squeeze it together.

2. Wrap each roll in aluminum foil and place on a tray. Place a baking sheet on top of the rolls and weigh it down with a heavy plate or cans. Refrigerate for at least 4 hours and up to 1 day. Serve at room temperature.

This is a sort of oversize sandwich that's quite delicious. It's also best eaten with a knife and fork. For a crispier bread, bake the loaves closer to the heat source. If it's chewy bread you're after, bake it on the middle rack.

Serves 4

Fennel Flatbread with Tomatoes, Mozzarella, Sausage, and Arugula

1	package dry active yeast
	Pinch of sugar
1½	cups warm water (about 85°F)
1	large egg, lightly beaten
3	tablespoons extra-virgin olive oil, plus extra for brushing
4½	cups bread flour
½	teaspoon baking soda
1½	teaspoons sea salt
2	tablespoons fennel seeds, crushed
	Coarse cornmeal
	Freshly ground black pepper to taste
1½	cups diced plum tomatoes (about ½ pound)
¾	cup shredded fresh mozzarella cheese (about 3 ounces)
4	cooked fennel sausages, cut into ¼-inch slices
2	cups arugula leaves, torn into bite-size pieces
8	oil-cured olives, chopped

1. Dissolve the yeast and sugar in the warm water in a large mixing bowl. Set aside for 5 minutes.

2. Stir in the egg and 2 tablespoons of the olive oil. Beat in 2 cups of the flour, the baking soda, salt, and fennel seeds. Beat in enough additional flour to form a soft and sticky dough.

3. Remove the dough from the bowl and knead on a floured surface for about 10 minutes, until it is smooth but still slightly sticky. While kneading the dough, sprinkle the surface with just enough of the remaining flour to keep the dough from sticking. Lightly oil the mixing bowl and place the dough in the bowl, turning to coat the surface with oil. Cover and let rise for 30 minutes, or refrigerate the dough overnight.

4. Preheat the oven to 475°F. Place a piece of parchment paper on each of 2 baking sheets, brush with oil, and sprinkle the paper with cornmeal.

5. Divide the room temperature dough into 4 equal pieces and shape into 4 balls. Roll each into an 8-inch circle. Brush the surface with olive oil and lightly season the top with pepper. Bake for 15 minutes, or until golden brown. Remove from the oven and cool for 5 minutes.

6. Mix together the tomatoes, cheese, sausage, and arugula in a medium-size mixing bowl. Season the mixture with salt and toss it with the remaining 1 tablespoon of olive oil.

7. Slice the bread lengthwise and place one half on each of 4 dinner plates. Spoon the tomato-sausage mixture over the bottom halves of the bread and top with the olives. Place the tops of the bread over the olives and serve immediately.

Is there anything more classic than a BLT? Try this version, with fried green tomatoes, for a whole new flavor experience. We like to keep some of the tradition the same, though, and so we proudly use old-fashioned white bread. All of the fancy seeded European-style breads are wonderful, but for this dish we like to stick to our roots. In the old days, our favorite beverage to go with the sandwiches was a frosty mug of root beer. That, or an ice-cold beer, still works on a hot summer day.   **Serves 2**

BLT with M, Fried Green Tomato Style

4	thick slices bacon
½	cup coarse cornmeal
1	teaspoon sea salt
½	teaspoon freshly ground black pepper
1	large green tomato, cored and thickly sliced
4	slices sturdy white bread
2	tablespoons mayonnaise
1	4-ounce ovalini mozzarella ball, sliced ⅓ inch thick
4	leaves romaine lettuce

1. Place the bacon strips in a medium-size skillet and fry them until crisp. Drain the bacon on paper towels and set aside. Return the skillet to the stove and place it over very low heat.

2. Stir together the cornmeal, salt, and pepper, and lightly dredge the tomato slices in the mixture. Sauté the tomatoes in the skillet over medium-low heat until golden brown, about 5 minutes per side. Remove from the heat and drain on paper towels.

3. Toast the bread until golden. Spread 2 slices of toast with 1 tablespoon each of the mayonnaise. Top each piece with the sliced cheese, the fried tomatoes, 2 bacon slices, and 2 lettuce leaves. Top with the other 2 pieces of toast. Slice and serve immediately.

Tea-Time Tomatoes and Mozzarella

The triple tomato butter in these mini sandwiches is a beautiful coral color. For a fancier look, cut the bread into 2½-inch rounds with a biscuit cutter. And by all means, use the tomato butter for more than just these tasty tea sandwiches. Spread it on toast to accompany your morning eggs, or use it as a sandwich spread instead of mustard or mayonnaise. A small pat atop a cheeseburger, veggie burger, or turkey burger with fresh tomatoes is scrumptious.

Makes 16 tea sandwiches

Tea Sandwiches with Mozzarella and Triple Tomato Butter

Triple Tomato Butter

8 ripe cherry tomatoes, halved

½ cup shredded fresh mozzarella cheese (about 2½ ounces)

½ tablespoon store-bought prepared sun-dried tomato pesto

½ tablespoon tomato paste

½ cup (1 stick) unsalted butter, at room temperature

8 slices thin white bread, crusts removed

½ English cucumber, unpeeled and very thinly sliced

4 medium-size ripe tomatoes (about 1 pound), thinly sliced

4 ounces bocconcini mozzarella balls, thinly sliced

1. To make the triple tomato butter, place the cherry tomatoes in the bowl of a food processor and pulse until pureed. Add the shredded mozzarella, the tomato pesto, and the tomato paste and pulse into a thick paste. Cut the butter into ½-inch pieces and add to the mixture. Pulse into a smooth spread.

2. Spread 1 tablespoon of the butter on each of the bread slices. Divide the cucumber slices over 4 slices of the bread. Top with the sliced tomatoes and sliced bocconcini. Cut the sandwiches into quarters and place on a serving platter. Serve at room temperature or slightly chilled.

Any proper tea should really include a platter of these charming buttery biscuits. For variety, spread some of the biscuits with cheese and tomatoes, and the rest with Triple Tomato Butter (at left) or Ginger Tomato Jam (page 116). Serve a classic afternoon tea such as Darjeeling with both a pitcher of warm milk and a bowl of small lemon wedges. If you can't find Sweet 100s, use the smallest grape or cherry tomatoes you can find. **Makes about 36 biscuits**

Mozzarella Angel Tea Biscuits with Sweet 100s

1	tablespoon active dry yeast
2	teaspoons sugar
¼	cup warm water
4	cups unbleached all-purpose flour
2	tablespoons store-bought prepared sun-dried tomato pesto
2	teaspoons baking powder
1	teaspoon baking soda
1½	teaspoons sea salt
1	cup (2 sticks) cold unsalted butter, cut into ½-inch pieces
1	cup milk (low-fat okay)
½	cup sour cream (low-fat okay)
1	large egg, beaten
18	bocconcini mozzarella balls (about 2¼ pounds), halved
3	dozen small Sweet 100 tomatoes, halved

1. Preheat the oven to 375°F. Line a baking sheet with parchment paper and lightly oil it or spray it with nonstick cooking spray.

2. In a small bowl, dissolve the yeast and sugar in the warm water. Place the flour, pesto, baking powder, baking soda, and salt in the bowl of a food processor. Pulse just to mix. Add the butter and pulse to incorporate into a pebbly texture. Remove the mixture to a large bowl and stir in the milk and sour cream to form a soft dough.

3. Turn the dough out on a floured surface and knead until smooth, about 1 minute. Roll the dough into a ¼-inch-thick rectangle and cut out 2½-inch circles using a biscuit or cookie cutter. Place the circles on the prepared baking sheet and brush with the beaten egg. Bake for about 20 minutes, or until the biscuits are golden brown. Remove from the oven and cool on a rack.

4. Split each biscuit in half lengthwise and fill with 2 tomato halves and a bocconcini half. If necessary, keep the biscuits closed with toothpicks. Serve at room temperature.

Here is the ultimate in no-brainer wonderful appetizers. Prepared puff pastry is so easy to work with, and there are many good brands available in the frozen-food section of your grocery store. Keep the assembled dough in the freezer and bake it at the last minute for a quick tea accompaniment, hors d'oeuvre, or salad garnish. **Makes 24 palmiers**

Tea Tomato Palmiers

1 sheet packaged puff pastry

⅔ cup store-bought prepared sun-dried tomato pesto

12 grape tomatoes, halved

24 ciliegine mozzarella balls (about 8 ounces)

1. Preheat the oven to 375°F.

2. Unroll the pastry sheet and flatten it slightly with a rolling pin. Spread the pesto over it liberally, leaving a ¼-inch border around the edges. Fold the dough into 3 layers by folding the top and bottom of the pastry sheet together over the center section. Fold it in half again lengthwise. Place the pastry in the freezer for 15 minutes.

3. Cut the pastry into twenty-four ¼-inch-thick slices and place them on an ungreased baking sheet. Bake for 15 minutes, or until golden brown. Allow to cool, then top each with a tomato half and a bocconcini. Secure with toothpicks and serve warm or at room temperature.

We first sighted these scrumptious tartlets in the windows of a fancy bakery in Paris, but they're easy to make at home. The translucent basil is beautiful as well as being a crunchy treat. These tartlets are particularly easy if you purchase frozen puff pastry sheets pre-cut into squares, which are now widely available in supermarkets. If you can't find them, buy puff pastry sheets and cut them to size. The puffy tartlets are so light, they seem to rise over the plate.

Makes 8 tartlets

Flaky Tomato Tartlets with Mozzarella and Crackly Basil

8 5-inch puff pastry squares, thawed according to package directions (about 1 pound)

½ cup store-bought prepared sun-dried tomato pesto

5 medium-size ripe tomatoes, thickly sliced

1 large bunch basil, stemmed

2 tablespoons canola oil

16 bocconcini mozzarella balls

1. Preheat the oven to 450°F. Lightly oil 2 baking sheets.

2. Arrange the pastry squares on the baking sheets. Spread each square of pastry with 1 tablespoon tomato pesto and top the pesto with 2 slices of tomato, slightly overlapping and placed on the diagonal. Bake on the center rack for 15 minutes, or until golden brown.

3. While the tartlets bake, place the basil leaves on a paper towel, brush with the canola oil, and microwave 1 to 2 minutes, or until crispy. When the tartlets are done, remove them to a cooling rack and top each with 2 bocconcini, one on either side of the tomatoes. Place 1 or 2 crackly basil leaves on top of each tart. Serve warm or at room temperature.

Ruby red and dark mahogany Cherokee Purple heirloom tomatoes are as sweet as candy and as juicy as ripe watermelon, and we like to use them for this jam when we can get them. In the Prescott, Arizona, farmers' market, we often get a little overinspired and end up buying bushels of tomatoes just because all the varietals are so colorful and promising. This jam originated from one of those tomato-buying frenzies and is a delicious tea-time treat with toasted bread rounds and fresh mozzarella, or as a filling in a tiny buttery biscuit. The left-over jam will keep, refrigerated, for up to one month.   **Makes 20 crostini**

Mozzarella Crostini with Ginger Tomato Jam

Ginger Tomato Jam

2½ pounds ripe tomatoes, peeled (see page 78) and coarsely chopped

1 cup water

4½ cups sugar

Zest of 1 medium-size orange

¼ cup fresh lemon juice

2 tablespoons peeled and minced fresh ginger

1 tablespoon minced preserved or candied ginger

1 small vanilla bean, halved lengthwise

1 day-old baguette, cut into twenty ¼-inch slices

2 tablespoons unsalted butter, melted

20 thin slices fresh mozzarella cheese (about 6 ounces)

1. Combine the tomatoes, water, sugar, orange zest, lemon juice, fresh ginger, and preserved ginger in a large heavy saucepan. Bring to a simmer over medium heat. Reduce the heat to medium-low and simmer for 30 minutes.

2. Add the vanilla bean and continue simmering for another 40 minutes, or until the jam has thickened. The temperature of the jam should be 220°F when an instant-read thermometer is inserted into it. Remove from the heat, discard the vanilla bean, and store in four 1-cup or two 1-pint jars.

3. Preheat the oven to 375°F. Place the baguette slices on a baking sheet and brush with the melted butter. Bake for 10 minutes or until lightly browned and toasted. Remove from the oven and cool slightly.

4. Place a slice of mozzarella on each piece of toast and top with a heaping teaspoon of the jam. Place the crostini on a large serving platter and serve immediately.

If you have fond memories of high tea from a trip to England, here's the simplest way to bring them back. Our modern version is lighter than the traditional cream scones, since we've substituted milk for the heavy cream. Serve them when they are still fairly warm. Slice each scone through the middle, spread with Triple Tomato Butter (page 110), add a small slab of the freshest mozzarella you can find, and top with a slice of just-picked heirloom tomato.

Makes 8 scones

Tomato Basil Tea Scones

1 cup quick-cooking rolled oats

1½ cups all-purpose flour

2 tablespoons sugar

2 teaspoons baking powder

½ teaspoon salt

1 teaspoon dried basil

7 tablespoons cold unsalted butter, cut into small pieces

1 large egg plus 1 egg yolk

½ cup milk (low-fat okay)

1 tablespoon tomato paste

1. Preheat the oven to 425°F. Line a baking pan with parchment paper and lightly oil it or spray it with nonstick cooking spray.

2. Place the oats, flour, sugar, baking powder, salt, and basil in a food processor and pulse to combine. While the machine is running, add the butter and pulse to incorporate completely. The butter will give the mixture a cornmeal-like texture.

3. In a small bowl, stir together the egg and egg yolk, milk, and tomato paste. Again, while the food processor is running, add the egg mixture and pulse just until the dough forms a sticky mass. Using a spatula, remove it from the bowl and form an 8-inch circle on the prepared pan. Moisten your hands with water to make it easier to spread the dough.

4. Bake for 18 to 20 minutes, or until golden brown. Remove, allow to cool slightly, and cut into 8 large wedges.

This creamy variation on classic eggplant caviar is best made by hand. You can use a food processor, but if you do, watch it carefully! The texture should remain slightly chunky. The blini are adapted from a recipe we first tasted at the Petrossian caviar boutique in Paris. The slight amount of buckwheat flour is just enough to give the pancakes a hint of the classic without being overbearing. Make the batter a day ahead, if you wish, keeping the egg whites aside. Just before cooking the blini, whip the whites and whisk them into the batter.

Serves 12

Eggplant and Mozzarella Mousse with Silver Dollar Tea Blini

1 medium-size globe eggplant (about 1 pound)

1 teaspoon olive oil, plus extra for drizzling

1 small head garlic

½ teaspoon *herbes de Provence*

1 large store-bought roasted red pepper, julienned

1 medium-size ripe tomato, cored and diced

1 green onion, thinly sliced (green part only)

2 tablespoons minced fresh cilantro leaves

2 teaspoons minced fresh basil leaves

½ teaspoon ground cumin

Sea salt and freshly ground pepper to taste

2 tablespoons fresh lemon juice

1 teaspoon red wine vinegar

Scant 1 cup diced fresh mozzarella cheese (about 4 ounces)

Silver Dollar Tea Blini (at right)

Additional olive oil (optional)

1. Preheat the oven to 350°F.

2. Slash the eggplant in several places with a knife and rub it lightly with a little of the olive oil. Place it on a baking sheet. Slice ½ inch from the top of the garlic bulb and place it on a sheet of aluminum foil. Drizzle the garlic with the remaining olive oil and sprinkle it with the *herbes de Provence*. Wrap up the bulb in the foil and place it on the baking sheet. Roast the eggplant and garlic until soft, 45 minutes to 1 hour. Remove from the oven and allow to cool slightly.

3. Remove the garlic skins and peel the eggplant. Squeeze the pulp from the garlic onto a chopping board. Finely mince the eggplant and garlic pulp along with the red pepper, tomato, green onion, cilantro, basil, cumin, salt, and pepper. Sprinkle the lemon juice and vinegar over the mixture and blend. Place the mixture in a medium-size bowl and stir in the mozzarella.

4. Spread a generous tablespoon of the mixture on each warm blini. If you wish, drizzle the tops of the blini with additional olive oil.

Silver Dollar Tea Blini

Makes about 24 blini

1 cup whole milk
1 teaspoon active dry yeast
1 tablespoon sugar
¾ cup unbleached white bread flour
2 tablespoons buckwheat flour
2 eggs, separated
2 tablespoons unsalted butter, softened to room temperature
¼ teaspoon salt

1. Place the milk in a medium-size saucepan and heat over medium heat just to a simmer. Remove from the heat, cool to 80°F, and transfer to a large mixing bowl. Stir in the yeast and sugar. Beat in the bread and buckwheat flours. Cover the bowl with plastic wrap and set aside for 1 hour to let the batter rise.

2. After the batter has risen, mix in the egg yolks, butter, and salt. Beat well to combine. Cover the bowl again and let the dough rise for 1 hour, or refrigerate for up to 1 day.

3. When you are ready to make the blini, whisk the egg whites until stiff and gently fold into the batter. Heat a greased griddle or nonstick skillet over medium-high heat. Ladle 2 tablespoons of the batter onto the griddle and brown about 1 minute on each side. Repeat until all the batter is used, and keep the cooked blini warm in a low oven.

Here's how to wow 'em. This savory adaptation of a classic Italian dessert is different and fun. A tidy and elegant little tea-time or cocktail treat, it is a perfect addition to any festive gathering. The unfilled cannoli shells can be kept in an airtight container at room temperature for several days or frozen for up to one month, then filled shortly before serving. If you can't find Golden Romas, use regular red plum tomatoes instead. **Makes 12 cannoli**

Parmesan Cannoli Filled with Golden Romas and Bocconcini

1 cup diced Golden Roma heirloom tomatoes (about 5 ounces)

½ cup diced fresh mozzarella cheese (about 2 ounces)

1 tablespoon minced fresh basil leaves

1 large garlic clove, minced

1 tablespoon red wine vinegar

1 teaspoon extra-virgin olive oil

Sea salt and freshly ground pepper to taste

4 cups grated Parmesan cheese

1. Mix together all the ingredients, except the Parmesan cheese, in a large bowl.

2. Heat a small lightly oiled nonstick skillet over medium heat. Spread ⅓ cup of the Parmesan cheese in an even layer on the bottom of the skillet. Cook until the cheese melts together and forms a solid cake, about 2 minutes. The bottom will be light golden brown. Remove it from the skillet and quickly form the cheese into a cylinder around a cannoli tube, a small wooden dowel, or a thin rolling pin.

3. Repeat with the remaining Parmesan cheese, oiling or spraying the skillet again as necessary.

4. As the cannoli shells cool, gently remove them from the forms. Fill each shell with 2 generous tablespoons of the tomato-mozzarella mixture. Serve immediately.

Pasta Pomodori

We have Mama May Pino-Acquaro, Shelley's mother, to thank for this easy and mouthwatering recipe, which is made with cornmeal rather than with potatoes. May, the matriarch of Shel's family, taught us all the joys and pleasures of good, simple Italian fare. Feel free to quickly warm the marinara, covered, in the microwave for one to two minutes. We're sure she'd approve of the shortcut!

Serves 4 to 6

Roman-Style Gnocchi

3 cups whole milk

1 cup yellow cornmeal

2 large eggs, beaten

5 tablespoons unsalted butter, at room temperature

1 teaspoon salt

Pinch of freshly ground black pepper

2 cups shredded mozzarella cheese

2 cups Marinara Sauce (page 139), warmed

1. Generously oil a 13 × 9-inch baking pan. Heat the milk in a large saucepan over medium heat until it is just beginning to simmer. Gradually whisk in the cornmeal and cook for about 5 minutes, stirring frequently, until thickened. Stir in the eggs, 3 tablespoons of the butter, the salt, the pepper, and 1 cup of the mozzarella cheese. Spoon into the prepared pan and let the mixture cool completely, about 30 minutes.

2. Preheat the oven to 400°F.

3. Cut the cornmeal mixture into 2-inch squares and place in an ungreased baking pan. Dot the surface with the remaining 2 tablespoons of butter, and sprinkle the remaining 1 cup mozzarella over the top. Bake, uncovered, for 35 minutes, or until bubbly. Serve topped with the warmed marinara sauce, or with a bowl of it alongside, in Mama May's style.

Here's a super supper in 30 minutes. If you're feeding the football team, rest assured that the recipe doubles, triples, and then some. Even spicy-food skeptics will be happy with this, as the mild cheese balances all the heat from the sausages and chiles. By the way, should you have any leftover roast pork on hand, feel free to substitute it for the sausage or add it to the sausage mixture.

Serves 2

Spicy Tagliatelle with Hot Pepper Oil and Mozzarella

2 hot Italian sausage links (about 5 ounces), thinly sliced, *or* 5 ounces Italian-style roast pork, cubed

1 tablespoon olive oil

1 large garlic clove, thinly sliced

1 14-ounce can diced tomatoes with green chiles

Sea salt and freshly ground black pepper to taste

8 ounces dried tagliatelle

1 cup shredded mozzarella cheese

1 tablespoon store-bought hot pepper olive oil

1/3 cup grated Parmesan cheese

1. In a large skillet, brown the sausages in the oil over medium heat. Add the garlic and sauté for 1 minute. Stir in the tomatoes and reduce the heat to medium low. Simmer for 25 minutes, or until the sauce has thickened.

2. While the sauce simmers, fill a large pot with salted water and heat to boiling. Add the pasta and boil until *al dente*. Drain and pour the noodles back into the pot.

3. Add the sauce and mozzarella to the noodles and stir quickly to combine. Add the hot pepper oil and stir again. Pour immediately into a large serving dish. Sprinkle the Parmesan cheese over the top and serve immediately.

Despite its fiery name, this is not a spicy dish; rather, the mound of noodles with fresh tomato sauce and molten mozzarella resembles a volcanic eruption. This sauce benefits in flavor from being made a few days ahead, making it great for casual entertaining. Open a hearty red wine to accompany this pasta, and pass a big bowl of Parmesan cheese at the table.

Serves 4

Pasta Vesuvio

2	large garlic cloves
1	shallot, halved
6	medium-size ripe tomatoes, cored and quartered
3	tablespoons extra-virgin olive oil
1	tablespoon minced fresh oregano
½	teaspoon salt
¾	pound fettuccine
⅔	cup grated Parmesan cheese
2½	cups diced fresh mozzarella cheese (about ½ pound)
2	tablespoons minced fresh basil

1. Place the garlic and shallot in the bowl of a food processor and pulse until finely minced. Add the tomatoes and pulse until coarsely pureed.

2. In a large skillet, heat the olive oil over high heat. Add the tomato mixture, oregano, and salt. When the mixture boils, reduce the heat to medium-low and simmer for 20 minutes.

3. While the sauce cooks, boil the pasta in salted water just until tender. Drain, reserving 1 cup of the cooking water, and place the pasta in a large serving bowl. If the sauce appears to be too thick, add a small amount of the pasta water to thin it, then toss the sauce with the pasta. Stir in both cheeses and the basil. Cover the dish with foil for a few minutes so that the mozzarella begins to melt. Serve immediately.

A well-done classic risotto is creamy and luscious. Just imagine it with fresh, milky, and silky-soft mozzarella added. It's heaven for Italian-food lovers! True, it requires some attention and time at the stove, but it's very easy work. This vegetarian rice dish is a satisfying first course. Follow it with a small portion of grilled fish or, in the dog days of summer, a room-temperature roasted chicken salad. **Serves 4 to 6**

Creamy Tomato and Mozzarella Risotto

1 tablespoon extra-virgin olive oil

3 tablespoons unsalted butter

1 cup Arborio rice

1 medium-size yellow onion, chopped

2 garlic cloves, thinly sliced

3 cups homemade or store-bought vegetable broth, heated to boiling

4 cups chopped plum tomatoes (about 1½ pounds)

1 cup shredded fresh mozzarella cheese (about 4 ounces)

3 tablespoons grated Parmesan cheese

1. Heat the oil and 1 tablespoon of the butter in a large saucepan. Add the rice and sauté for 3 minutes. Stir in the onion and garlic and sauté for 2 minutes. Add the broth 1 cup at a time, stirring frequently until the broth has evaporated before adding more. Before adding the second cup of broth, stir in the tomatoes.

2. After the last cup of broth has been added, let the liquid evaporate completely, then stir in the cheeses and the remaining 2 tablespoons butter. Mix thoroughly to melt the cheeses and serve immediately.

As much as we adore the convenience of no-boil lasagna noodles, the old-fashioned kind work best here. The others fail to absorb the sauce thoroughly and remain downright crunchy. This can be made ahead and cooked, then frozen and thawed, with great results. Or assemble the lasagna, cover, and freeze for up to three months. Let it thaw overnight in the refrigerator and then bake. A crisp green salad and a glass of Chianti, and maybe a ripe fall pear afterward, are all that's needed for this dinner.   **Serves 4**

Tomato and Mozzarella Lasagna

5 ounces lasagna noodles

2 generous cups shredded mozzarella cheese

5 tablespoons extra-virgin olive oil

1 pound large plum tomatoes, each cored and cut into 12 to 14 thin lengthwise slices

3 garlic cloves, minced

2 tablespoons store-bought prepared sun-dried tomato pesto

1 cup grated Parmesan cheese

1 cup garlic-herb bread crumbs

3 ounces prosciutto

1. Heat a large pot of salted water to boiling and parboil the noodles for 2 to 3 minutes. Drain and set aside. While the water is heating, mix together the shredded mozzarella and 2 tablespoons of the olive oil in a large bowl.

2. Stir the tomatoes, garlic, pesto, and ½ cup of the Parmesan into the mozzarella. Oil a 9-inch-square pan and place a layer of noodles on the bottom. Spoon in ⅓ of the cheese filling and dust the top with 2 tablespoons of the bread crumbs. Cut the prosciutto slices in half crosswise and place 2 halves over the bread crumbs.

3. Make two more layers of pasta, filling, bread crumbs, and prosciutto; all the filling should be used up after the third layer. Finish with a layer of pasta. Sprinkle the remaining ½ cup Parmesan cheese and the remaining bread crumbs over the top. Drizzle the remaining 3 tablespoons olive oil over the top. Cover and refrigerate for 4 to 6 hours to soften and mellow the lasagna.

4. Preheat the oven to 425°F. Bake the lasagna, uncovered, for 30 to 40 minutes, or until nicely browned on top. Let sit for a few minutes before serving.

Orecchiette, or "little ears," pasta makes a fast and delicious summer salad. Both the roasted and sweet fresh tomatoes and the olives get caught in the hollows of the pasta and give the dish an intense flavor. This is a great picnic or cookout dish, as it can be made several hours ahead.

Serves 8

Pasta Salad with Roasted Tomatoes, Mozzarella, and Oil-Cured Olives

¾ pound plum tomatoes, cored and halved

½ cup olive oil

¼ cup red wine vinegar

1 tablespoon capers

1 garlic clove, minced

1 pound orecchiette

2 cups chopped ripe tomatoes (about ¾ pound)

2½ cups diced fresh mozzarella cheese (about ½ pound)

1 cup tightly packed fresh basil leaves, thinly sliced

1 cup grated Parmesan cheese

½ cup pitted oil-cured black olives, minced

Sea salt and freshly ground black pepper to taste

1. Preheat the oven to 300°F.

2. Place the halved tomatoes on an oiled baking sheet and drizzle with 2 tablespoons of the olive oil. Bake for 45 minutes to 1 hour, until the tomatoes have softened and become lightly browned. Remove from the oven and cool slightly.

3. Place the remaining 6 tablespoons of olive oil, the vinegar, capers, garlic, and roasted tomatoes in a food processor and pulse 3 or 4 times until the tomatoes are coarsely chopped. Place the mixture in a small bowl and set aside.

4. Cook the pasta in large pot of boiling salted water, stirring occasionally, until *al dente*. Drain the pasta and transfer it to a large serving bowl. Stir the roasted tomato mixture into the hot pasta. Cool the dish completely, stirring occasionally to blend the flavors.

5. Gently stir in the chopped fresh tomatoes, mozzarella, basil, Parmesan, and olives. Season to taste with salt and pepper. Cover and chill for up to 6 hours. Allow to come to room temperature before serving.

On the streets of Naples, you'll find outdoor cafés serving this flat omelet at lunchtime and very late at night. It's one of our favorite light suppers after the theater or a movie. Buy salted butter for this, and have a potato peeler handy. It's a perfect tool for shaving the cheese. Use a regular box grater for the tomato.

Serves 4

Southern Italian Pasta Omelet

½ pound spaghetti

3 tablespoons salted butter

6 large eggs, beaten

⅓ cup kalamata olives, pitted and coarsely chopped

2 tablespoons olive oil

2 tablespoons milk (low-fat okay)

1 large ripe tomato, halved and grated

1 4-ounce ovalini mozzarella ball, cubed

1 teaspoon sea salt

½ teaspoon lemon pepper

Shavings of Parmesan cheese for garnish

1. Bring a large saucepan with salted water to a boil and cook the pasta just until *al dente*. Drain, place it back in the pot, and stir in the butter. Set aside.

2. In a medium-size bowl, stir together all the remaining ingredients except the Parmesan. Lightly oil a medium-size skillet. Place the pasta in the skillet and brown one side over medium heat. Pour in the egg mixture and reduce the heat to medium-low. Cook until the eggs are barely set, 5 to 7 minutes.

3. Heat the broiler to high and broil the omelet for 1 minute. Scatter the Parmesan shavings over the top and serve immediately from the skillet.

If you live in an area where winter brings snowfall, this is the comfort food to make during one of those blustery storms. If you've never added cinnamon to tomatoes and beef before, you'll be amazed at how delicious the combination is. This is rich and hearty enough so that a small green salad, a sturdy glass of red wine, and a welcoming fire are all you need to round it out. **Serves 4 to 6**

Beefy Mac 'n' Cheese

3 tablespoons unsalted butter

3 tablespoons flour

1 quart milk (low-fat okay)

½ medium-size onion, chopped

¼ teaspoon ground nutmeg

⅛ teaspoon ground cinnamon

1 pound elbow-shaped pasta

1 pound ground beef

3 cups shredded mozzarella cheese

1 cup shredded Gruyère cheese

2 cups chopped ripe tomatoes (about 10 ounces)

⅔ cup grated Parmesan cheese

⅓ cup bread crumbs

2 tablespoons olive oil

1. Preheat the oven to 375°F. Oil a 13 × 11-inch casserole dish and set aside.

2. Melt the butter in a large soup pot over medium heat and whisk in the flour, stirring for 1 minute. Stir in the milk, onion, nutmeg, and cinnamon and reduce the heat to medium-low. Cook for 15 to 20 minutes, stirring occasionally. The sauce will be fairly thin.

3. Boil the pasta in salted water according to the package directions. Brown the meat in a large frying pan. Drain the noodles and add them to the sauce along with the meat, 2 cups of the mozzarella, the Gruyère, and the tomatoes. Combine this mixture thoroughly.

4. Place half of the mixture into the prepared baking dish. Top with ½ cup of the mozzarella and then another layer of pasta. Top the dish with the remaining ½ cup mozzarella.

5. In a small bowl, mix together the Parmesan cheese and the bread crumbs and sprinkle the mixture over the top of the casserole. Drizzle the oil over the top and bake for 20 to 25 minutes, or until bubbly. Serve piping hot.

Use a variety of wild mushrooms in this sophisticated yet still comforting baked pasta dish. If you can find cèpes, morels, or trumpet mushrooms, by all means use them! However, oyster and cremini mushrooms are more accessible and work wonderfully here.   **Serves 4**

Wild Mushroom Macaroni and Cheese

4	tablespoons unsalted butter
3	tablespoons all-purpose flour
1	quart milk (low-fat okay)
	Pinch of cayenne pepper
1	pound pasta, such as rotini or penne
4	tablespoons olive oil
1	garlic clove, minced
1	pound wild mushrooms, coarsely chopped
1	tablespoon minced fresh Italian parsley
3	cups shredded mozzarella cheese
1	cup shredded Gruyère cheese
2	cups chopped ripe tomatoes (about 10 ounces)
²/₃	cup grated Parmesan cheese
¹/₃	cup bread crumbs

1. Preheat the oven to 375°F. Oil a 13 × 11-inch casserole dish and set it aside.

2. Melt 3 tablespoons of the butter in a large soup pot over medium heat and whisk in the flour, stirring for 1 minute. Stir in the milk and cayenne and reduce the heat to medium-low. Cook for 15 to 20 minutes, stirring occasionally. The sauce will be fairly thin.

3. While the sauce cooks, boil the pasta in salted water according to the package directions. Drain the pasta and stir it into the sauce. Heat 2 tablespoons of the olive oil and the remaining 1 tablespoon butter in a large skillet over medium heat and sauté the garlic for 30 seconds. Add the mushrooms and cook for 8 to 10 minutes, until softened. Remove from the heat and stir in the parsley. Stir the mushrooms, 2 cups of the mozzarella, the Gruyère, and the tomatoes into the pasta and combine thoroughly.

4. Place half of the mixture into the prepared baking dish. Top with ½ cup of the remaining mozzarella and then another layer of noodles. Top the dish with the remaining ½ cup mozzarella.

5. In a small bowl, mix together the Parmesan and bread crumbs and sprinkle it over the top of the casserole. Drizzle the remaining 2 tablespoons olive oil over the top and bake for 20 to 25 minutes, or until bubbly. Serve hot.

On first glance, these seafood roll-ups look somewhat complicated. All the elements are easy, though, and each one can be made ahead for use when you are ready. Even the noodles can be cooked in advance, then lightly oiled and refrigerated. The only thing to make at the last minute is the fresh seafood mixture. The final assembly takes only minutes. If you can find them, do give canned organic fire-roasted plum tomatoes a try in this sauce. Their slightly rustic, charred flavor is a welcome contrast to the richer, more refined, creamy white sauce.

Serves 3 as a main course or 6 as a first course

Winter Seafood Lasagnetti

2	tablespoons olive oil
1	large shallot, minced
1	small carrot, chopped
1	stalk celery, chopped
1	tablespoon minced fresh ginger
1	large garlic clove, minced
1	14.5-ounce can peeled tomatoes with their juice
2	teaspoons tomato paste
½	cup white wine
6	sheets lasagna noodles
1	tablespoon salted butter
1	tablespoon all-purpose flour
½	cup heavy cream
1	tablespoon fresh lemon juice
	Sea salt and freshly ground black pepper to taste

½	pound shrimp, shelled, deveined, and coarsely chopped
½	pound sea scallops
1	tablespoon brandy or cognac
1	small bunch green onions, coarsely chopped (about 4 to 6 thin onions)
1½	cups shredded mozzarella cheese

1. Preheat the oven to 375°F. Oil a 9-inch-square pan or oval baking dish.

2. Heat the olive oil in a large skillet and sauté the shallot, carrot, celery, ginger, and garlic for 3 minutes, or until softened. Stir in the tomatoes and their juice, the tomato paste, and the wine and reduce the heat to a simmer. Cook for 15 minutes.

3. Boil the noodles in a large pot of salted water for about 5 minutes, or until the noodles begin to float on the surface of the pot. Drain and set aside.

4. When the sauce is ready, cool it slightly and then place it in a food processor or blender and puree until smooth. Melt the butter in the skillet over medium heat and stir in the flour. Cook for 2 minutes, and then stir in the tomato sauce and cream. Cook the sauce for an additional 2 minutes, then stir in the lemon juice and season lightly with salt and pepper. Remove the sauce from the heat and set aside.

5. Place the shrimp, scallops, brandy, green onions, and ½ cup of the mozzarella in a food processor and pulse into a chunky puree. Transfer to a small bowl.

6. To bake the lasagnetti, place ½ cup of the sauce in the prepared baking dish. Place ½ cup of the fish mixture on 1 end of each noodle and roll the noodle around the filling. Place the filled noodles over the sauce and top them with the remaining sauce. Bake for 30 minutes. Remove from the oven and set the oven temperature to broil. Sprinkle the remaining 1 cup mozzarella over the top of the dish and broil for 3 to 4 minutes, until bubbly and browned. Let it sit for a few minutes before serving.

Although these shells are more American in origin than Italian, the marinara, pesto, ricotta, and mozzarella speak to every Little Italy around the nation. Using turkey rather than traditional beef or veal in the filling makes the manicotti lighter and suitable as a first course. If you do want to serve this as an appetizer, follow the pasta with a simple roasted chicken with rosemary, little stuffed tomatoes, and a simple green salad dressed with olive oil and lemon.

Serves 4

Turkey Manicotti with Marinara and Mozzarella

¾ pound manicotti shells

¾ pound ground turkey

1 cup ricotta cheese

2 cups shredded mozzarella cheese

1 tablespoon store-bought prepared sun-dried tomato pesto

Sea salt and freshly ground black pepper to taste

3 cups Marinara Sauce (at right) or store-bought marinara sauce

1. Preheat the oven to 375°F. Oil a 13 × 11-inch ovenproof baking dish and set aside.

2. Place the manicotti shells in a large pot of boiling salted water and parboil for 5 minutes. Drain and set aside to cool.

3. Place the turkey, ricotta, 1 cup of the mozzarella, and the pesto in a large bowl and mix thoroughly. Season lightly with salt and pepper and mix well again.

4. Pour 2 cups of the marinara sauce into the bottom of the prepared baking dish. Using a small spoon, place 1 tablespoon of the turkey-cheese filling in each end of the shells. Place the filled shells in the dish, side by side. When all the shells have been filled, pour the remaining marinara sauce over the top and sprinkle the remaining 1 cup mozzarella over the sauce.

5. Cover with foil and bake for 20 minutes. Uncover and bake for an additional 15 minutes, or until the manicotti are bubbly. Remove and let them sit for 5 minutes before serving.

Marinara Sauce

Makes 3 cups

In the dead of winter, a vibrant red sauce can wake up your palate. This simple recipe will do the trick. Be sure to puree the sauce well; it's best with no chunks or lumps. Be advised that some brands of plum tomatoes are sold in very thin juice. If needed, you can add up to 1½ cups of canned tomato sauce to thicken it. Also, feel free to double or triple the amounts and freeze whatever you have left over for up to two months.

 1 tablespoon olive oil
 2 large garlic cloves, minced
 1 28-ounce can plum tomatoes with basil, with their juice
 ½ cup dry white wine
   Sea salt and freshly ground black pepper to taste

Heat the olive oil in a large skillet over medium heat. Add the garlic and sauté for 1 minute. Stir in the tomatoes, breaking them up with a wooden spoon or spatula. Add the wine, reduce the heat to medium-low, and cook for 15 minutes, or until slightly thickened. Taste the sauce and season with salt and pepper to taste. Remove the sauce from the heat and allow it to cool slightly. Pour it into a blender and puree into a smooth sauce.

Main Events

Tians are traditional rustic Provençal casserole dishes that are ovenproof and pretty enough to bring right to the table. (As with "casserole," *tian* also refers to the food in the dish.) A regular oval gratin or casserole dish is also just fine for this. The eggplant technique, given to me by author Mary Evans, was a complete revelation. Boiling the eggplant removes all bitterness, eliminates the need to salt it, and saves lots of time and oil that usually goes into frying. The mild eggplant devours the flavor from the sauce and is soft, succulent, and delicious. Like all respectable casseroles, this can be assembled up to two days in advance and baked before serving.

Serves 4

Tian of Eggplant and Tomatoes

1 medium-size eggplant (about 1 pound), sliced ¼ inch thick

2 tablespoons olive oil

1 medium-size fennel bulb, fronds trimmed and thinly sliced

1 large onion, chopped

2 garlic cloves, minced

Sea salt and freshly ground black pepper to taste

3 large tomatoes, cored and coarsely chopped

1 cup chopped fresh basil

4 large eggs, beaten

1 cup shredded fresh mozzarella cheese (about 3 ounces)

½ cup pitted kalamata olives

1. Preheat the oven to 375°F. Oil a 10-inch oval tian, gratin dish, or ovenproof skillet.

2. Heat a large pot of salted water to boiling. Drop the eggplant slices into the water and boil for 5 minutes. Remove the eggplant with tongs, place the slices on a paper towel, and pat dry.

3. In a large skillet, heat the olive oil over medium heat. Add the fennel, onion, and garlic. Season with salt and pepper and sauté for 5 minutes, or until the onion has softened. Add the tomatoes and cook for 7 to 8 minutes. The tomatoes will release their juice and the liquid will evaporate. Stir in ½ cup of the basil and remove from the heat.

4. Line the bottom of the prepared pan with eggplant slices. Top with the tomato mixture and pour the eggs over the top. Bake for 20 minutes. Remove from the oven and top with the cheese, olives, and the remaining ½ cup basil. Bake for an additional 20 minutes. Serve hot or at room temperature.

What could be more inviting than a homemade pizza, right out of the oven, with soft, gooey mozzarella and homemade marinara? This is the classic, Neapolitan bare-bones pizza, with only a basil sprig for decoration. The good news is that it's stunning and elegant in its simplicity and with just a few ingredients creates a perfect evening for friends. Semolina flour can be found in Italian markets and large supermarkets. In a pinch, you can use regular flour. Traditionally, fresh mozzarella is used for this particular pizza, but you may also use packaged shredded mozzarella.

Makes two 12-inch pizzas

Pizza Margherita

For the pizza dough

1	cup warm water (about 110°F)
	Pinch of sugar
1	package active dry yeast
1	teaspoon salt
2	tablespoons olive oil
2¼ to 2½	cups all-purpose flour
2	tablespoons semolina flour

2	cups Marinara Sauce (page 139) or store-bought marinara sauce
2	large ripe tomatoes, thinly sliced
8	ounces thinly sliced fresh mozzarella cheese or 2 cups shredded mozzarella cheese
2	large fresh basil sprigs

1. To make the pizza dough, in a large mixing bowl, mix together the water, sugar, and yeast. Let the mixture proof for 5 minutes, then stir in the salt and olive oil. Gradually add 2 cups of the all-purpose flour to form a soft and very sticky dough. Turn the dough out onto a floured surface and gradually incorporate up to ½ cup more flour to make a soft, supple, and only slightly sticky dough. Oil the mixing bowl and put the dough back in the bowl, turning the dough to coat the surface with oil. Cover and let rise for 45 minutes. Then gently push down the dough to release the air and cover and let rise for another 30 minutes.

2. Preheat the oven to 425°F. Oil 2 parchment paper–lined baking sheets or pizza pans and sprinkle each with 1 tablespoon semolina flour.

3. Divide the dough into 2 equal pieces and roll each into a 12-inch circle. Place the circles on the prepared sheets. Spread 1 cup of marinara sauce on each pizza. Top with the tomatoes and cheese.

4. Bake for 25 to 30 minutes, or until golden brown and bubbly. Remove from the oven and place 1 sprig of basil on each pizza. Cut and serve immediately.

Here's a niçoise pizza straight from the French-Italian border. We enjoyed this served on paper plates in a small outdoor café near the flower market in Nice. The line is never short, as people come to buy either a slice or two or whole pizzas to take away. In the United States, we love to make this with the tiny ciliegine mozzarella and Sweet 100s, the small cherry tomato. The mozzarella balls and tomatoes are about the same size and make for a beautiful presentation on top of the onions. If you don't wish to make your own dough, many supermarkets sell good-quality fresh pizza dough in the refrigerated section.

Makes two 12-inch pizzas

Caramelized Onion Pizza with Ciliegine and Sweet 100s

2	tablespoons butter
2	tablespoons olive oil
3	pounds yellow onions, thinly sliced
1	teaspoon sugar
	Sea salt and freshly ground black pepper to taste
2	teaspoons red wine vinegar
2	tablespoons semolina flour
	Pizza Dough (page 143)
6	ounces Sweet 100 or grape tomatoes
12	ounces ciliegine mozzarella balls, halved
3	tablespoons grated Parmesan cheese

1. Heat the butter and olive oil in a large saucepan over medium-high heat. Add the onions and stir to coat. Reduce the heat to medium-low, cover the skillet, and cook for 10 minutes, or until the onions have softened. Remove the cover, add the sugar, and season lightly with salt and pepper to taste. Simmer for 35 to 40 minutes, or until the onions are a rich golden brown. Remove from the heat and stir in the vinegar. Let the mixture cool.

2. Preheat the oven to 425°F. Oil 2 parchment paper–lined baking sheets or pizza pans and sprinkle each with 1 tablespoon semolina flour.

3. Divide the pizza dough into 2 pieces. Roll each into a 12-inch circle, place on the sheets, and spread the onion mixture over the dough. Arrange the tomatoes and mozzarella cheese in an alternating pattern over the onions.

4. Bake for 25 to 30 minutes, or until the pizza is golden brown and bubbly. Remove and sprinkle 1½ tablespoons Parmesan cheese over each pizza. Cut and serve immediately.

Think of this recipe when you are invited to a potluck party. The joy of this dish is that it can be made up to two days in advance and reheated before serving. It's great with a simple salad of fresh greens dressed with lemon juice and olive oil. Grilling the eggplant gives it a smoky touch, but it's also great if you oven broil it. Let the lasagna sit for at least 15 minutes before serving to re-absorb any juices that the tomatoes release during baking.   **Serves 8**

Layered Polenta Lasagna with Tomatoes and Mozzarella

3	tablespoons extra-virgin olive oil
2	tablespoons fresh lemon juice
3	tablespoons store-bought prepared sun-dried tomato pesto
2	small globe eggplants, sliced ½ inch thick
	Sea salt and freshly ground pepper to taste
5	cups water
1	cup milk (low-fat okay)
1	large garlic clove, minced
2	teaspoons salt
2	cups coarse cornmeal or polenta
¼	cup (½ stick) unsalted butter
1	cup grated Parmesan cheese
3	large ripe beefsteak tomatoes, sliced ½ inch thick
½	pound fresh mozzarella cheese, sliced ¼ inch thick

1. Prepare a hot fire in a grill, or preheat the oven to 475°F.

2. In a small bowl, whisk together the olive oil, lemon juice, and pesto. Season the eggplant with salt and pepper and grill or bake the slices for 8 to 10 minutes per side, brushing with the pesto mixture as they cook. Remove from the oven and set aside.

3. Reduce the oven temperature to 400°F. Oil a 13 × 9-inch lasagna pan.

4. In a large saucepan, bring the water, milk, garlic, and salt to a boil. Reduce the heat to a simmer and whisk in the polenta, along with 2 tablespoons of the butter. Cook for 10 to 12 minutes, stirring frequently, until the polenta has thickened and is fully cooked. Stir in the remaining 2 tablespoons butter and ½ cup of the Parmesan cheese.

5. Pour about half of the polenta into the prepared baking pan. Top with the sliced tomatoes, followed by the mozzarella, and finally the eggplant. Top the dish with the remaining polenta and ½ cup Parmesan cheese. Drizzle on any remaining marinade and bake for 30 minutes. Cool slightly before serving.

Although the cooking time may seem long for this dish, slow roasting allows all the individual flavors to intermingle. The potatoes melt and become tender, the onions become marvelously sweet, and the spices are mellowed. The smoked cheese adds a meaty quality, so although this is a great side dish for grilled poultry and pork, it is also substantial enough to serve as a hearty vegetarian meal. If you can find the hybrid Chilipeño chile, by all means use it here. It's hot like a jalapeño but has the softer texture of an Anaheim pepper. **Serves 6**

Slow-Roasted Smoked Mozzarella and Vegetable Casserole

2	large onions, thinly sliced
2	large garlic cloves, minced
3	tablespoons extra-virgin olive oil
1	pound crookneck squash, cut into 1/3-inch rounds
1/2	pound small red potatoes, cut into 1/4-inch rounds
3	large ripe tomatoes, cored and coarsely chopped
1	each red and green bell pepper, cored, seeded, and cut into 1-inch squares
1	Chilipeño chile or jalapeño chile, seeded and minced
6	ounces white mushrooms, sliced 1/4 inch thick

1	tablespoon fresh thyme leaves
1	tablespoon fresh basil leaves
3/4	cup white wine
1 1/2	cups shredded smoked mozzarella cheese (4 ounces)
1/2	cup grated Parmesan cheese

1. Preheat the oven to 350°F.

2. Oil a roasting pan and place the onions and garlic in the pan. Coat the vegetables with the olive oil. Cover the pan with foil and roast for 30 minutes.

3. Remove the pan from the oven and add all the remaining ingredients except for the 2 cheeses. Cover the pan again and bake for 1 hour. Uncover the dish, sprinkle with the mozzarella and Parmesan cheeses, and bake for 20 minutes, or until the cheese has melted. Serve hot or warm.

A few years ago we were a big part of the tomato festival at the beautiful Farm at South Mountain in Phoenix, Arizona, which grows more than 30 varieties of tomatoes. We created this humble dish in honor of the event. We think it's actually better if assembled and refrigerated overnight before baking. That way the broth absorbs into the bread and the result is almost like a savory bread pudding.

Serves 6

Spring Tomato and Bread Casserole

2 tablespoons extra-virgin olive oil

2 large sweet onions, thinly sliced

3 large garlic cloves, minced

Sea salt and freshly ground black pepper to taste

½ loaf rustic country bread (about 8 ounces) at least 1 day old, sliced and toasted

2 tablespoons minced fresh basil leaves

2 tablespoons minced fresh Italian parsley

4 medium-size ripe tomatoes, cored and sliced ¼ inch thick

½ cup grated Parmesan cheese

3 to 4 cups homemade or store-bought vegetable broth, as needed

4 ounces fresh mozzarella cheese, thinly sliced

1. Preheat the oven to 375°F.

2. In a large skillet, heat the olive oil over medium heat and sauté the onions for 5 minutes. Stir in the garlic and cook for 1 minute. Season with salt and pepper.

3. Oil a large gratin or casserole dish. Make 2 layers each of the onions, bread, herbs, and tomatoes. Top the second layer of tomatoes with the Parmesan cheese. Slowly pour 3 cups of the broth around the edges. Drizzle a little oil over the top of the dish, cover, and bake for 45 minutes.

4. Uncover the dish and bake about 20 minutes more, or until the top is just starting to brown. Remove it from the oven, spread the mozzarella on top, and bake for an additional 15 minutes, or until the gratin is well browned and the cheese is melted and light brown speckled. If the dish seems at all dry, add up to 1 cup more broth and bake for another few minutes. Let stand for 15 minutes at room temperature before serving.

Long, hot summer days quickly give way to fall weather, and often we're still left with bushels of tomatoes that will never have a chance to ripen. That's the time to pull out this handy recipe. We love the balance of the hot chorizo and chiles against the mild pancake-like topping; it helps to put out the spicy fire. Depending on your taste buds, feel free to adjust the heat by using more or fewer chiles.

Serves 6

Spicy Fried Green Tomato and Mozzarella Pie

For the filling

½	pound chorizo sausage, casings removed and chopped
2	cups fresh or defrosted frozen corn kernels
2	green onions, chopped
1	small Chilipeño, jalapeño, or serrano chile, stemmed, seeded, and minced
1	large red bell pepper, stemmed, seeded, and diced
¼	cup all-purpose flour
3	tablespoons fine cornmeal
½	teaspoon sea salt
2	cups chopped green tomatoes (about 10 ounces)
3	tablespoons olive oil
1	cup shredded mozzarella cheese

For the topping

¾	cup fine cornmeal
2	tablespoons all-purpose flour
½	teaspoon sea salt
½	teaspoon freshly ground black pepper
1	teaspoon dried thyme
2	eggs
½	cup milk (low-fat okay)

1. Preheat the oven to 425°F. Oil a 1-quart oval or square baking dish.

2. In a large skillet, brown the chorizo over medium heat for 5 minutes. Drain on paper towels, and place in the prepared baking dish. Add the corn to the dish and stir to combine.

3. Remove all but a small film of oil from the skillet. Add the onions and the chile and bell peppers and sauté over medium heat for about 5 minutes, or until the vegetables have softened. Place on top of the chorizo-corn mixture, but do not mix.

4. In a large bowl stir together the flour, cornmeal, and salt. Add the tomatoes and stir to coat thoroughly. Wipe out the skillet, add 2 tablespoons of the olive oil, and sauté the tomatoes over medium heat until browned on all sides, about 10 minutes. Remove and place in the baking dish. Top with the cheese.

5. To make the topping, stir together the cornmeal, flour, salt, pepper, and thyme in a medium-size mixing bowl. In a small bowl, mix together the eggs and milk, and then stir the egg mixture into the dry ingredients. Beat well and pour the mixture over the pie. Drizzle the remaining tablespoon of olive oil over the top. Bake for 20 to 25 minutes, or until golden brown. Cool for 10 minutes before serving.

The late Michael James, author of *Slow Food* (Time Warner Books, 1992), was well known for his unique lobster pot pie. He inspired the divinely rich yet simple biscuit crust on our tomato pot pie. Using ripe, luscious yellow tomatoes results in a pie that is both chic and homey, evoking memories of Sunday suppers all across America.   **Serves 4**

Rich Tomato Pot Pie

For the crust

1	cup all-purpose flour
1/4	teaspoon salt
5	tablespoons unsalted butter
3	tablespoons whipping cream
1	large egg

For the filling

1	cup snap peas
3	small tender carrots, diced
2	tablespoons olive oil
1	medium-size onion, chopped
	Sea salt and freshly ground black pepper to taste
2	large garlic cloves, minced
3	large red tomatoes, cored, halved, and grated against the side of a box grater
1/2	teaspoon dried thyme
4	medium-size portobello mushrooms, chopped

2	large ripe yellow tomatoes, thickly sliced
4	ounces fresh mozzarella cheese, thinly sliced
1	large egg mixed with 1 teaspoon whipping cream

1. To make the crust, place the flour, salt, and butter in the bowl of a food processor and pulse until the mixture resembles fine crumbs. In a small bowl, mix together the cream and egg. With the machine running, add the liquid, and process until the dough just holds together. Remove the dough from the bowl, dust lightly with flour, and press into a 6-inch disk. Wrap in plastic and refrigerate while preparing the filling.

2. To make the filling, fill a large saucepan with water, add a generous pinch of salt, and heat to boiling. Have a bowl of very cold water nearby. Plunge the snap peas into the boiling water and cook for 30 seconds, until the peas turn bright green. Remove with a slotted spoon to the cold water. Add the carrots to the boiling water and cook for 2 minutes. Remove to the cold water. Drain the snap peas and carrots in a colander.

3. In a large skillet, heat the olive oil over medium heat and sauté the onion for 5 minutes, seasoning with salt and pepper. Stir in the garlic, red tomatoes, and thyme and simmer for 15 minutes, or until the juice from the tomatoes has evaporated. Remove ½ cup of the sauce and set aside. Add the mushrooms to the skillet and simmer for 5 minutes.

4. Preheat the oven to 400°F. Lightly oil a 9-inch soufflé or casserole dish.

5. Spread the reserved sauce over the bottom of the dish. Scatter the onions, carrots, and peas over the sauce and top with the tomato-mushroom mixture. Cover the surface with the yellow tomatoes and cheese.

6. Remove the dough from the refrigerator and roll out on a lightly floured surface to a scant ¼ inch thick. Place on top of the baking dish and crimp the edges. Slash the dough in 3 or 4 places to allow steam to escape. Brush the top with the egg mixture and bake for 30 minutes, or until golden brown. Serve immediately.

Although this tart is crustless, it bakes up nice and crusty in the oven! It's great year round and can be served hot or at room temperature, and also can be assembled ahead and baked at the last moment. It's substantial enough to be a main course, but also makes a tasty side dish alongside roasted or grilled meats. French-style green beans, also called *haricots verts,* are found in most supermarkets these days. Along with the listed vegetables, feel free to add or substitute any other cooked vegetables you may have on hand—carrots, peppers, and zucchini work well.

Serves 4

Potato Tart with Green Beans, Tomatoes, and Mozzarella

½ pound French-style green beans

1 pound red potatoes, peeled and sliced ¼ inch thick

1 cup fresh bread crumbs

¾ cup milk (low-fat okay)

2 tablespoons olive oil, plus more for drizzling

2 large cloves garlic, minced

1 tablespoon minced fresh marjoram

3 tablespoons minced fresh Italian parsley

2 cups chopped plum tomatoes, with their juice (about 10 ounces)

½ cup grated Parmesan cheese

½ cup ricotta cheese

1 cup shredded mozzarella cheese

5 large eggs, beaten

1. Heat the oven to 350°F. Oil a 9-inch oval or round baking dish.

2. Place the green beans in a medium-size pan of boiling water and blanch for 2 to 3 minutes. Remove with a slotted spoon and set aside to drain. When cool, chop the beans.

3. Bring the water back to boiling, add the potatoes, and simmer for 20 minutes, or until very tender. Drain and place them in a large bowl. Coarsely mash the potatoes and set aside.

4. Place the bread crumbs in a small bowl and stir in the milk. Set aside.

5. Heat 2 tablespoons of the oil in a medium-size skillet over medium heat and sauté the garlic for 1 minute. Add the green beans, marjoram, and parsley, and cook for 1 minute. Remove from the heat and place the mixture in a large bowl. Stir in the potatoes, tomatoes, Parmesan, ricotta, ½ cup of the mozzarella, and the eggs. Transfer the mixture to the baking dish, evening it out with a spatula. Pat the soaked bread crumbs onto the top of the dish and sprinkle the remaining ½ cup of mozzarella over the crumbs. Bake until golden brown, 35 to 40 minutes.

6. Let cool for 10 minutes before serving, or allow to cool to room temperature. Serve in the dish with a cruet of olive oil alongside, if desired.

These stuffed chiles, which we serve with steaming rice alongside, have become one of our favorite main courses. They are also good without the rice as a first course. The secret is to parboil the poblanos before stuffing them. Often, those wonderful peppers can be too hot. It's hard to tell when choosing them, so parboiling ensures that although they will still be piquant, your taste buds will remain intact.

Serves 4

Stuffed Poblano Chiles with Tomato-Avocado Salsa

Tomato-Avocado Salsa

4   medium-size avocados, peeled, pitted, and diced

4   cups diced plum tomatoes (about 1½ pounds)

2   serrano chiles, seeded and minced

2   large shallots, minced

2   large garlic cloves, minced

¼   cup fresh lime juice

¼   cup minced fresh cilantro

8   large poblano peppers

1   cup shredded mozzarella cheese

1. Mix together all of the salsa ingredients in a large bowl. Set it aside. If not using the salsa immediately, cover and refrigerate for up to 2 days.

2. Prepare a hot fire in a grill or preheat the broiler. Bring a large pot of salted water to a boil and add the peppers. Boil for 3 minutes, drain, and refresh in cold water. Cut a ¼-inch slice from the stem top and set aside. Carefully remove the seeds from the pepper, keeping each poblano whole. Fill each seeded pepper with 1 ounce of the cheese and place on an oiled baking sheet.

3. Place the stem tops on the peppers and grill or broil them until slightly charred. Check to see that the cheese has melted. Spread the salsa on a large serving platter and place the peppers on top. Serve immediately.

This recipe features a mighty-flavored chili oil that goes well with anything you're grilling. Try it with tuna, chicken, turkey, summer vegetables like eggplant and zucchini, and of course with grilled, beefy, ripe heirloom tomatoes. (For a great side, grill eggplant and zucchini slices while you're grilling the salmon.) On Sunday mornings, try brushing a little bit of the oil over a cheese omelet for a spicy finish. The chili oil will keep for a month refrigerated in a clean glass container.

Serves 4

Southwestern Grilled Salmon with Tomato-Chili Oil

Tomato-Chili Oil

1	large ripe tomato, chopped
2	garlic cloves, smashed
¼	teaspoon New Mexico chili powder
1½	cups olive or canola oil

1	pound salmon fillets, cut into 4 pieces
	Sea salt and freshly ground black pepper to taste
2	generous cups shredded fresh mozzarella cheese (about ½ pound)

1. Place the tomato-chili oil ingredients in a medium-size pot over low heat. Cook until the oil is almost simmering and beginning to bubble around the edges, 5 to 7 minutes.

2. Cool the oil and strain, pressing down on the solids, into a clean wide-mouth jar or bottle.

3. Prepare a hot fire in a grill.

4. To make the salmon, season the salmon fillets with salt and pepper and grill for 3 minutes. Turn the fillets over and sprinkle the cheese over the top. Close the lid and grill for 3 minutes more, until the cheese has melted. Remove the salmon to a serving platter and brush the tomato-chili oil generously over the top. Serve immediately.

We developed this easy and elegant fish dish for Shelley's local TV show in Phoenix. We had more requests for this dish than we could have ever hoped for! It's quick to assemble and can be made in any season, as long as you can obtain really fresh fish. Serve with rice.

Serves 4

Hearts and Sole

1	pound sole fillets (6 to 8 fillets)
4	ounces prosciutto
4	ounces fresh mozzarella cheese, cut into 8 thin slices
¾	cup almonds
3	tablespoons salted butter, melted
1	tablespoon olive oil
1	cup finely chopped green onions (white and green parts)
1	6.5-ounce jar marinated artichoke hearts
1	cup chopped plum tomatoes (about 5 ounces)
2	tablespoons white wine

1. Preheat the oven to 375°F. Oil a baking sheet.

2. Place the sole fillets on a cutting board. Cut the prosciutto slices in half lengthwise and place on top of the fillets, dividing them equally among the fillets. Top the prosciutto with the cheese slices, and roll the fish into packets.

3. Place the almonds in the bowl of a food processor and grind them finely. Place the crumbs on a dinner plate and roll each fish packet in the crumbs. Place the fish rolls on the prepared baking sheet and drizzle 2 tablespoons of butter over the tops. Bake for about 15 minutes, or until the fish is firm.

4. While the fish cooks, heat the olive oil in a large skillet and sauté the green onions for 1 minute. Add the artichokes, tomatoes, and wine and cook for 5 minutes. The tomatoes will retain their shape, and the artichokes should be warmed through. Whisk in the remaining tablespoon of butter and simmer for 2 minutes.

5. Place the fish packets on a large, warm serving platter and spoon the sauce over and around them. Serve immediately.

These quick-to-make quesadillas can be prepared with both white and dark meat. A store-bought roasted chicken is just fine, or use leftover chicken from another meal. The salsa is easily made and keeps for up to 10 days in the refrigerator, making this a quick and nutritious dinner on the run.

Makes 8 quesadillas

Chicken Mozzarella Quesadillas with Smoky Tomato Salsa

Smoky Tomato Salsa

1½	cups diced plum tomatoes (about ¾ pound)
½	cup fresh corn kernels
2	canned chipotle peppers in adobo sauce, minced
1	jalapeño chile, stemmed, seeded, and minced
½	small red onion, diced
2 to 3	tablespoons fresh lime juice
1	tablespoon olive oil
½	cup chopped fresh cilantro
	Sea salt to taste

4	cups cooked shredded chicken
8	8-inch flour tortillas
¾	cup shredded mozzarella cheese
2½	tablespoons canola oil

1. To make the salsa, place the tomatoes, corn, chipotle peppers, jalapeño chile, red onion, lime juice, olive oil, and cilantro in a large bowl. Season with salt, blend, and set aside for 30 minutes.

2. Preheat the oven to 375°F.

3. To assemble the quesadillas, place ½ cup of the shredded chicken on the bottom half of each tortilla. Top each one with ¼ cup of the salsa and 2 tablespoons of the mozzarella. Fold the tortillas in half to form half-moons.

4. Place the quesadillas on a baking sheet and brush the tops with canola oil. Bake for 10 minutes, or until the cheese melts. Spoon the remaining salsa over the quesadillas, or serve the additional salsa on the side, and serve immediately.

The need for a quick summer Sunday lunch after shopping in the farmers' market in San Francisco inspired this no-fuss crowd pleaser. If you are using a charcoal grill, the dish can be fully assembled and ready to cook in the time it takes the charcoal to heat. Serve with crusty bread and a crisp and slightly spicy dry white wine. A bowl of cool, fresh peaches would be a welcome finish.

Serves 4

Grilled Chicken-Mozzarella Paillards with Grilled Tomatoes and Greens

8 boneless, skinless chicken thighs

Sea salt and freshly ground black pepper to taste

4 fresh sage leaves

3 ounces fresh mozzarella cheese, thinly sliced into 8 rounds

8 large escarole leaves

1 tablespoon fresh lemon juice

2 tablespoons extra-virgin olive oil

2 large firm beefsteak tomatoes, sliced ⅓ inch thick

1. Prepare a hot fire in a grill.

2. Working with two pieces of chicken at a time, place the chicken between two pieces of plastic wrap and pound them to ¼ inch thick. Remove the plastic, turn the chicken over, and season the undersides with salt and pepper. Place a sage leaf on 4 of the thighs. Place 2 small slices of cheese over the sage leaves. Top each with another thigh to create a "sandwich." Press the ends well to seal them. Season the tops of the chicken with salt and pepper.

3. Place the escarole leaves in a large bowl. Whisk together the lemon juice and olive oil and pour over the escarole. Toss to coat.

4. Place the tomatoes on the grill and cook until slightly charred, about 5 minutes. Turn and grill until the underside is slightly charred. Remove to a large serving platter.

5. Grill the chicken for 5 minutes on each side. After you turn the chicken, add the escarole leaves to the grill and cook just until wilted. Place the chicken and greens on the platter next to the tomatoes and serve immediately.

Native to southern Italy, this cheese-filled chicken dish is good hot or at room temperature. The sauce makes itself as the chicken cooks. It's light, thin, and filled with flavor from the chicken. A little of the cheese might ooze out while it bakes. If it does, all the better! It crisps beautifully under the broiler. Serve with a side of pasta and a green salad. **Serves 4**

Neapolitan-Style Stuffed Chicken

½ medium-size yellow onion, sliced

2 large garlic cloves, thinly sliced lengthwise

1¼ pounds plum tomatoes, sliced lengthwise into eighths

Sea salt and freshly ground black pepper to taste

4 skinless, bone-in chicken thighs

1 4-ounce ovalini mozzarella ball, cut into quarters

4 sun-dried tomato halves in olive oil

1. Preheat the oven to 350°F. Oil a medium-size ovenproof baking dish and place the onion slices in the bottom. Scatter the garlic over the onion, and top with the tomato slices. Season lightly with salt and pepper.

2. Lightly season the underside of the chicken with salt and pepper. Place 1 piece of cheese and 1 sun-dried tomato half on each chicken thigh. Fold over and place in the dish on top of the tomato-onion mixture. Brush the tops of the chicken thighs with 1 tablespoon of the oil from the sun-dried tomatoes, and lightly season the tops with salt and pepper.

3. Bake for 1 hour. Remove the chicken from the oven and turn the oven to broil. Broil the chicken for 3 minutes, or until slightly charred and crispy on top. Serve hot or at room temperature.

Although this dish is traditionally made with veal, when we experimented with turkey, we loved the texture and lighter flavor. Thin pork cutlets can also be substituted and cooked in exactly the same way. The whole dish can be assembled ahead and baked at the last minute, and if time is really short, store-bought marinara or spaghetti sauce can be substituted for homemade.

Serves 4

Baked Scaloppine with Eggplant, Tomatoes, and Mozzarella

¼ cup olive oil
1 large globe eggplant, cut into ⅓-inch-thick slices
4 5-ounce turkey cutlets
2 tablespoons unsalted butter
¼ cup store-bought prepared basil pesto
1 garlic clove, minced
½ cup dry red wine
1 cup homemade or store-bought chicken broth
½ cup Marinara Sauce (page 139) or store-bought marinara sauce
4 ounces fresh mozzarella cheese, thinly sliced

1. Preheat the oven to 400°F. Lightly oil a 13 × 9-inch baking dish.

2. Pour 2 tablespoons of the olive oil onto a baking sheet and place the eggplant slices on the sheet. Turn to coat each one in the olive oil. Bake the slices for 20 minutes. Turn the eggplant slices over and bake for another 20 minutes. Remove the eggplant from the oven and set it aside to cool.

3. Place the cutlets between two pieces of plastic wrap and pound into ¼-inch slices. Heat 1 tablespoon of the olive oil and 1 tablespoon of the butter in a large skillet over medium-high heat. Brown the cutlets for 1 minute on each side. Remove to a large plate or baking sheet. Spread a generous 2 teaspoons of pesto over each cutlet and place them in the prepared pan.

4. Add the remaining tablespoon olive oil and the garlic to the skillet and sauté for 1 minute. Stir in the wine and bring to a boil. Cook until the liquid has evaporated, about 2 minutes, then add the broth, the remaining tablespoon of butter, and the marinara sauce. Cook over medium heat for 10 minutes.

5. Place the cutlets in the baking dish. Cover with ½ cup of sauce from the skillet. Top with the eggplant, mozzarella slices, and the remaining skillet sauce. Bake for 10 minutes. Let cool for 5 minutes, then serve immediately.

The versatile spicy chutney in this recipe is a bright accompaniment to both vegetarian and meat dishes. It's delicious spooned over scrambled eggs and is a fabulous alternative to mayonnaise on a sandwich of juicy tomatoes and mozzarella. The chutney keeps for a week in the refrigerator and can be made at any time of year. The recipe makes about one quart, allowing for great leftovers and experiments! Couscous is a wonderful accompaniment to this dish.

Serves 4

Grilled Pork Chops with Chunky Tomato Chutney

Chunky Tomato Chutney

1   28-ounce can plum tomatoes in tomato sauce with basil

1   large jalapeño chile, unseeded and minced

1   tablespoon minced fresh ginger

¼   cup extra-virgin olive oil

1   dried pasilla chile, unseeded and cut into 6 pieces

1   teaspoon ground cumin

1   teaspoon ground mustard

2   large garlic cloves, thinly sliced

½   cup golden raisins

½   cup rice vinegar

4   8-ounce loin pork chops

Sea salt to taste

1   cup shredded mozzarella cheese

1. To make the chutney, in a large bowl mix together the tomatoes, jalapeño, and ginger. Heat the olive oil in a large skillet over medium heat and sauté the pasilla chile pieces for 2 minutes, or until fragrant and slightly crispy. Stir in the cumin, mustard, and garlic and cook for 1 minute.

2. Stir in the tomato mixture, breaking the tomatoes up with a large spoon. Add the raisins and vinegar and cook for 15 minutes over medium-low heat. The oil may separate; this is fine, as it will emulsify later on. Remove from the heat and let the chutney cool.

3. While the chutney is cooking, prepare a hot fire in a grill.

4. Season the pork chops with salt and grill for 3 to 5 minutes on each side. Spread the mozzarella over the top of the pork and cover the grill for 30 to 45 seconds, or until the cheese has melted. Remove the pork immediately and serve with the chutney.

This stuffed pork tenderloin looks fabulous without a lot of effort and is great for serving a crowd. As the meat roasts, the mozzarella, which is tucked into the seam of the pork roll, melts into the meat, keeping the tenderloin as moist and tender as can be. This dish is even better if prepped and refrigerated one day before baking. The tomato-olive relish can be prepared ahead and kept in the refrigerator for up to three days. The relish would also be delicious on fish such as tuna or salmon, as a bread spread, or mixed with pasta. **Serves 4**

Stuffed Porchetta with Chunky Olive and Tomato Relish

2 ¾-pound pork tenderloins

1 tablespoon ground fennel

2 teaspoons sea salt

2 teaspoons freshly ground black pepper

2 garlic cloves, minced

3 ounces fresh mozzarella cheese, cut into ¼-inch strips

Chunky Olive and Tomato Relish (at right)

1. Using a sharp knife, butterfly each tenderloin by slicing the meat lengthwise, leaving both halves connected. In a small bowl mix together the fennel, salt, pepper, and garlic. Sprinkle both sides of the split tenderloins with the spices. Spread the cheese along the crease that holds the halves together. Fold over to form the tenderloin into one piece and tie in 3 places with kitchen string. Refrigerate, uncovered, for at least 1 hour or up to 6 hours.

2. Meanwhile, make the Chunky Olive and Tomato Relish.

3. Preheat the oven to 375°F.

4. Place the pork on an oiled baking sheet and roast for 25 to 30 minutes, or until an instant-read thermometer registers 140°F when inserted into the center. Remove from the oven and brush any bits of melted cheese onto the top of the meat. Cut the tenderloin into ⅓-inch-thick slices and serve immediately, with the relish alongside.

Chunky Olive and Tomato Relish

Makes 2 cups

2   medium-size red tomatoes, coarsely chopped
¼   cup store-bought prepared sun-dried tomato pesto
¼   cup extra-virgin olive oil
    Zest and juice of 1 large lemon
¼   cup black olives of your choice, pitted and quartered
1   garlic clove, minced
¼   cup basil leaves, chopped
    Coarse salt and freshly ground pepper to taste

Mix all the ingredients together in a large bowl and set aside. Refrigerate
until a half hour before serving.

When fresh artichokes are in season, this southern Mediterranean dish must be on the menu. Sometimes it's tricky to remove the fuzzy inedible center of the artichokes. Using a melon baller makes it short work. Be sure to use a pan that will hold the artichokes snugly so that they don't topple over. If you wish, you may serve the artichokes on a bed of rice.   **Serves 4**

Oven-Braised Stuffed Artichokes

¾ pound ground lamb

⅓ cup chopped kalamata olives

1 tablespoon tomato paste

1 tablespoon minced fresh Italian parsley

1 tablespoon minced fresh mint leaves

1 4-ounce ovalini mozzarella ball, cut into ¼-inch cubes

Sea salt and freshly ground black pepper to taste

2 large ripe beefsteak tomatoes, sliced ¼ inch thick

1 medium-size yellow onion, chopped

1 garlic clove, thinly sliced

1 tablespoon olive oil

4 large globe artichokes

1 lemon, halved

½ cup homemade or store-bought chicken broth

1. Preheat the oven to 375°F.

2. Mix the lamb, olives, tomato paste, parsley, mint, and ½ cup of the mozzarella in a large bowl. Season the mixture lightly with salt and pepper and set aside.

3. Place the tomatoes in the bottom of a medium-size ovenproof saucepan. Sprinkle the tomatoes with the onion, garlic, and olive oil and season lightly with salt and pepper.

4. Remove the stem and outer tough green leaves from each artichoke. Cut ¾ inch from the top, leaving a trimmed artichoke with pale green leaves. Rub the surface of each artichoke with the lemon halves to prevent them from discoloring. Carefully spread the leaves of each one and remove the fuzzy choke in the center.

5. Place the lamb mixture between the leaves and in the center of each artichoke, using a generous ½ cup filling for each one. There will be enough filling to mound the top of the artichoke. Set the filled artichokes over the tomatoes and pour the broth into the bottom of the pan.

6. Cover the pan with foil and bake for 50 to 60 minutes, until the artichoke leaves are very tender. Remove from the oven and dot the tops of the artichokes with the remaining cheese cubes. Re-cover with the foil and let sit for 5 minutes, or until the cheese has melted. Serve hot or warm.

The marriage of ginger, sun-dried tomatoes, and fresh tomatoes with mild-mannered beef tenderloin and mozzarella is a fetching combination. Roast the meat and make the vinaigrette a day ahead, then just before serving, slice the meat and cheese and spoon the dressing over everything. Serve it all up with thick slices of Italian bread. Use your favorite mild-flavored marinade for the tenderloin, if you wish.

Serves 4 to 6

Beef and Beefsteaks with Ginger Vinaigrette

2¼ pounds beef tenderloin

2 teaspoons minced fresh ginger

1 tablespoon store-bought prepared sun-dried tomato pesto

2 teaspoons Dijon mustard

2 teaspoons tomato paste

2 tablespoons cider vinegar

2 tablespoons fresh grapefruit juice

¼ cup olive oil

Sea salt and freshly ground black pepper to taste

1½ tablespoons water, if needed

1 pound fresh mozzarella cheese

3 large ripe beefsteak tomatoes

2 tablespoons slivered fresh basil leaves

1. Preheat the oven to 400°F.

2. Place the beef tenderloin in a roasting pan and bake for about 25 minutes. Cook until an instant-read thermometer inserted into the center reads 130°F for rare, 140°F for medium, 160°F for well-done, or according to your preference. Cover and set aside, or cover and refrigerate for up to 1 day.

3. In a medium-size bowl, whisk together the ginger, pesto, mustard, tomato paste, vinegar, and grapefruit juice. Whisk in the olive oil and season with salt and pepper. If the dressing appears too thick, thin it with up to 1½ tablespoons of water.

4. When ready to serve, slice the beef, cheese, and tomatoes ¼ inch thick on the diagonal and place them on a serving platter in an alternating pattern. Spoon the dressing over the top and scatter the basil over the platter. Serve slightly chilled or at room temperature.

Measurement Equivalents

Please note that all conversions
are approximate.

Liquid Conversions

U.S.	Metric
1 tsp	5 ml
1 tbs	15 ml
2 tbs	30 ml
3 tbs	45 ml
¼ cup	60 ml
⅓ cup	75 ml
⅓ cup + 1 tbs	90 ml
⅓ cup + 2 tbs	100 ml
½ cup	120 ml
⅔ cup	150 ml
¾ cup	180 ml
¾ cup + 2 tbs	200 ml
1 cup	240 ml
1 cup + 2 tbs	275 ml
1¼ cups	300 ml
1⅓ cups	325 ml
1½ cups	350 ml
1⅔ cups	375 ml
1¾ cups	400 ml
1¾ cups + 2 tbs	450 ml
2 cups (1 pint)	475 ml
2½ cups	600 ml
3 cups	720 ml
4 cups (1 quart)	945 ml (1,000 ml is 1 liter)

Weight Conversions

U.S./U.K.	Metric
½ oz	14 g
1 oz	28 g
1½ oz	43 g
2 oz	57 g
2½ oz	71 g
3 oz	85 g
3½ oz	100 g
4 oz	113 g
5 oz	142 g
6 oz	170 g
7 oz	200 g
8 oz	227 g
9 oz	255 g
10 oz	284 g
11 oz	312 g
12 oz	340 g
13 oz	368 g
14 oz	400 g
15 oz	425 g
1 lb	454 g

Oven Temperatures

°F	Gas Mark	°C
250	½	120
275	1	140
300	2	150
325	3	165
350	4	180
375	5	190
400	6	200
425	7	220
450	8	230
475	9	240
500	10	260
550	Broil	290

Index

2 1982 02119 0974